# Extraterrestrial Intervention
## The Evidence

Jacques Bergier and the Editors of *INFO*

HENRY REGNERY COMPANY • CHICAGO

**Library of Congress Cataloging in Publication Data**

Bergier, Jacques, 1912–     comp.
    Extraterrestrial intervention.

    Includes bibliographies.
    1. Curiosities and wonders.     I. The Info journal.
II.  Title.
AG243.B43      001.9'3      74–6884
ISBN 0-8092-8369-7

# CONTENTS

# PREFACE

Charles Fort is dead, but his work lives on. The influence of this singular and extraordinary man, who was born in 1874 and lived until 1932, can best be defined by his four books: *The Book of The Damned, New Lands, Lo!,* and *Wild Talents.*

In these books, he collected facts that were unwelcome to orthodox science. He was motivated by the spirit of the eternal student, but at the same time he performed a tremendous task by systematically researching the scientific magazines published from the beginning of the last century.

On January 26, 1931, a number of his admirers, including Theodore Dreiser, Booth Tarkington, Ben Hecht, Harry Leon Wilson, John Cowper Powys, Alexander Woollcott, Burton Rascoe, Aaron Sussman, and Tiffany Thayer founded the Fortean Society, with Tiffany Thayer acting as its secretary general. The society published a quarterly magazine, *Doubt.*

In 1959, Thayer died and the Fortean Society ceased to exist. The torch was picked up a few years ago by two young Americans,

Paul and Ronald Willis, who founded the International Fortean Organization (INFO). This group publishes a magazine called *The INFO Journal* (P.O. Box 367, Arlington, Virginia 22210). Many articles originally published in this magazine have been selected to form the present book, supplemented by a number of cases I have selected from other sources.

One of the chief goals of this book is to inform its readers about the world in which they live, a stranger world than they imagine. While the press and the mass media take note of events that are out of the ordinary, they are too ready to offer simplistic explanations.

For example, at the very moment these lines were being dictated, an adult wolf was captured near Meaux in France. The French press immediately explained that this wolf had traveled on foot from Poland. This is a reassuring but also fatuous explanation in view of the fact that Poland and France are separated by frontiers equipped with barbed wire and electric lines and protected by the most modern detectors, which an animal the size of a wolf would be completely unable to pass. The explanation of this event will perhaps be discovered one day—but by thinking about the problem, not by being lulled to sleep by completely impossible explanations.

Now I would like to ask the reader to think about and marvel at the extraordinary face of the universe. As Fort said, the following facts can be gathered merely by consulting serious scientific journals: "Red rain on Blankenberghe on November 2, 1819. Rain of mud in Tasmania on November 14, 1902. Snowflakes as large as saucers in Nashville on January 24, 1891. A rain of frogs in Birmingham on June 30, 1892. Meteorites. Balls of fire. Unexplained tracks in Devonshire in 1850. UFOs. 'Cupmarks' on stone. Machines in the sky. Caprices of comets. Strange disappearances. Inexplicable cataclysms. Inscriptions on objects fallen from the sky. Black snow. Blue moons. Green suns. Sudden showers of blood."

All these and many other things can be found in scientific magazines and in the reliable daily press. It is not possible to investigate every single case, but a certain number of cases can be selected and studied in depth. A number of attitudes can be assumed toward these phenomena that insolently seem to provoke us. Obviously we can systematically deny everything, as Lavoisier denied the existence of meteorites on the theory that: "Stones cannot fall from the sky because there are no stones in the sky."

This attitude is no cause for amusement; in that same sky, modern astronomers observed an explosion the fragments from which flew away from each other at a speed possibly greater than that of light. However, according to Einstein, relativity requires that the speed of light be an absolute limit.

Whether we like it or not, there are stones in the sky, and it seems clear that there exist speeds greater than that of light. We cannot systematically deny everything that is contrary to established knowledge. Moreover, denial is not a scientific attitude, as the scientists themselves say. By the same token, we cannot systematically accept every event. Everything must be verified with extreme care.

I shall give two examples, one classic, the other a contemporary example that is not well known. The first is Fontenelle's case of the child with the gold tooth. At the end of the seventeenth century, word spread that a child with a gold tooth had been born. People immediately asked whether this portended the end of the world or simply a major revolution in France. Fontenelle was sufficiently curious to go and look at the child. He found that the "tooth" was a thin gold film placed in the child's mouth by its parents. This did not prevent the French Revolution from occurring, but it is doubtful that it was caused by the child with the gold tooth.

The contemporary example is very significant because it shows how carefully verifications must be made in extraordinary cases. Some ten years ago, bones of prehistoric animals, particularly birds, dating from a million years ago, were discovered in catacombs under the city of Odessa in the Soviet Union. Close examination showed that there were spiral holes in them containing traces of iron and cobalt.

The seemingly obvious conclusion was that extraterrestrial visitors had taken samples with metal tools. This conclusion was made public, but with extreme prudence.

Continued research turned up a mollusk that digs spiral holes and whose blood contains iron and cobalt. This explanation seems simpler than that of an extraterrestrial intervention, and ultimately it was the one adopted. But if research had not been continued, proofs that would have been false would have attributed the holes to extraterrestrial intervention. Distrust, together with an open mind, are therefore indispensable.

There are many mysterious facts that yield to this approach, vanishing as soon as the light of research shines upon them. There is, for example, the case of the flying saucers. Careful investigations have proven beyond doubt that many claimed sightings have been hoaxes. This has also been true of materializations, ectoplasms, and other prodigies of the mediums, including levitating tables! When films have been made with infrared light during certain seances, the fraud has become apparent.

But a sufficient number of unexplained facts remain to supply material for quite a few books of this type. In the absence of explanations, we can at least try to classify them. A preliminary classification, necessarily simplified, consists of four categories, which has been observed in this book.

## 1.  Vanished civilizations

No one denies that civilizations have disappeared. In the words of the French poet Paul Valéry, "Civilizations are mortal."

However, what official science does energetically deny is the existence in the past of civilizations that were technologically as advanced or more advanced than ours. Yet we are constantly discovering objects that appear to come from such civilizations. Part One of this book is devoted to these discoveries.

## 2.  Extraterrestrial beings

It is statistically highly probable that extraterrestrial civilizations exist. It is not impossible that one or several of these civilizations could have intervened—or does intervene—on several occasions in the life of the human race. Certain phenomena of this type are described in Part Two.

## 3.   Unknown animals

Our earth has not been as thoroughly explored as has been claimed. Not only are discoveries made of dead and living specimens of species believed to be fossils and to have disappeared tens of millions of years ago, but occasionally traces are also discovered of completely unknown animals that cannot be classified among the fossils or among the known living species. Although these beings are not extraterrestrial, the clear evidence of their existence supports the theory of the existence of other life-forms than those that orthodox science recognizes. Part Three of this book deals with these apparitions.

## 4.   Extraordinary interventions in our daily lives

There is no doubt that our daily lives are disturbed by strange phenomena often called "visitations"—a very poor name for them. In other ages, this type of phenomenon was attributed to the spirits of the dead, to the gods, or to demons. In our day, we no longer propose to explain, but we try above all to classify and describe. Whatever the source of these interventions, their existence further supports the theory that forces do exist outside the sphere of ordinary perception. A certain number of these phenomena, selected for their authenticity and their dramatic nature, are the subject of Part Four.

Many of our readers will be able to acquaint us with "inexplicable"—or, more accurately, unexplained—facts they have observed, and which fall into one or another of these categories. For us, this is more than just a hope; it is practically a certainty, and one that fills us with enthusiasm.

**Jacques Bergier**

# PART ONE
## VANISHED CIVILIZATIONS

# THE ACAMBARO FIGURINES
## Ronald J. Willis

*The following article aroused general emotion throughout the world. It is, indeed, nothing less than a total disruption of our ideas about the past.*

*The Acambaro figurines are small statues that apparently were produced two thousand years ago;\* nevertheless they represent human beings, prehistoric animals, and animals that are completely unknown.*

*Instead of stating my personal opinion, I shall give that of the Soviet historian G. Buslaev, published in the magazine* Technology and Youth *(No. 10, 1971, page 56), together with the text of Ronald Willis's article and several photographs.*

*My own observations disregard the Soviet historian's argument that the capitalist government is responsible for the dispersal of this collection of figurines and the closing of an immense door opening onto the past.*

*The latest dates for these figurines are over 3600 B.C.—R.J. Willis

3

*This book is not political, and so I shall not argue with Mr. Buslaev. It is up to the Mexicans to protest if their government is accused of being capitalist. Let us remember that Mexico is both Catholic and Trotskyite, and that on Good Friday both Stalin and Judas are burned in effigy.*

*Mr. Buslaev admits the possibility that the Acambaro collection may be authentic and that some of the animals in question could have been inspired by prehistoric animals still existing at that time in Mexico.*

*Others were inspired by the alligator. A cult of the alligator existed in ancient Mexico, and alligators had been tamed in temples in the region. A woman straddling an alligator seems more plausible than a woman straddling a dinosaur. Under these conditions, the Acambaro figurines may be reminiscences, handed down from generation to generation and constantly reproduced, of a very distant past perhaps dating back twenty thousand years. This is the thesis of the Soviet historian, and I feel it is a very interesting one.*

In July 1945, Waldemar Julsrud, a businessman of Acambaro, Mexico, was riding on a hillside overlooking the town when he noticed some pottery fragments that had been washed out by the rainy season. Being interested in Mexican antiquities, he asked a local stonemason, Odilon Tinajero, to look into the site and bring him what he found. Tinajero apparently found much, for the collection made by Julsrud from 1945 to 1952 now comprises well over 30,000 pieces. Practically all archaeologists call them fakes, although hardly any have even bothered to *look* at them. But there is considerable reason to believe that this collection is one of the most amazing archaeological oddities in the world!

The illustrations in the photo insert show just a few of these figurines. Particularly disconcerting to the few archaeologists who have looked at the collection are the reptile figures. Some of these resemble dinosaurs and plesiosaurs. But since these creatures died out 70,000,000 years ago according to present theories, ancient

Mexican Indians couldn't know what they looked like. Modern people would, of course, through books and science-fiction movies.

One of the most fantastic facts about the whole collection is its amazing scope. There are no duplicates in over 30,000 pieces! There are similar pieces but no identical ones. The imagination that has gone into the production of all these "prehistoric" animals, humanoid figurines, "mummy figures," hundreds of tableaux in which often several animals and humans are acting out some story, etc., is simply staggering. Just the list of the types of objects found is lengthy.

*Types of objects found in the Julsrud collection*
1.  Tarascan pottery (a known and recognized Mexican Indian type)
2.  obsidian arrow and spear points—probably Tarascan
3.  teeth found with the figures—identified as *Equus Conversidens* Owen, an extinct Pleistocene horse
4.  several hundred bowls—not Tarascan—similar in material to the reptile statues
5.  a collection of masks
6.  numerous pipes—many of fantastic design
7.  the tableaux—showing animals and humans enacting some legend or story
8.  ceramic faces—never part of a larger figure
9.  coiled snakes
10. figures of mammals—many representing some Pleistocene animal such as rhinoceros, tapir, armadillo, extinct llama, etc.
11. flat plaques—with engraved designs of reptiles and other animals
12. ceramic objects imitating the bark of trees—but often with hidden pictures in the bark design
13. fishes and sea horses
14. large human statues—two to four feet high
15. "mummies"—six to ten inches high—*not* Egyptian looking

16.  large human and animal heads
17.  possible "Mayan" figures
18.  figurines suggesting Pacific culture contacts
19.  serpents or dragons
20.  a few jade bowls
21.  the reptile figurines—the largest category in the collection (uncounted thousands) many of which *suggest* Mesozoic reptiles but evidently do not *duplicate* them

plus thousands of miscellaneous objects, which may be musical instruments, etc., and many others that were unclassifiable

The current theory that the great reptiles died out 70,000,000 years ago and that modern man is only a recent development immediately rules out for most scientists the reptile figures and plaques that show man and these creatures together. And how would these Indians know of the woolly rhinoceros, American horses and camels, etc., which died out at the end of the Pleistocene age 10,000 to 12,000 years ago? Besides, the collection represents a knowledge and imagination broader than was ever known before the nineteenth century at the earliest. Many cultures have turned out artwork of marvelous quality and imagination, but no ancient culture ever turned out so many different things as the "Julsrud culture."

Figure three is a good example of this. There is a sort of dinosaur in the middle, a plesiosaur to the left, and a mask that in some ways resembles the Greek Gorgon masks between them. There are elephants above them, a figure to the far right that smacks of the ancient Near East, plus the row of "mummies" across the top shelf. Simply to describe the collection would take many volumes and a lifetime.

But if it were all a fake, why was it done? The collection took many years of hard work to make. Many objects such as the "mummies," the pipes, etc., are expertly made, incised, and *glazed*, which shows that an excellent artist was involved in their production. Julsrud paid Tinajero one peso for each complete figurine brought in. Sometimes these were broken and glued together. Julsrud never personally saw any of them dug up. If he paid Tinajero over 30,000 pesos for seven years of work, and the objects were fakes, the fakers were getting the short end of the deal. Thirty thousand pesos equals $3,600 (U.S.), or a little over $500 a year for all the fakers involved! They probably could have gotten more merely by exporting them as Mexican curios.

Investigators such as Professor Charles Hapgood were told at times by enemies of Julsrud that they knew of the "family" that made the objects in the town, but they could never supply any names or addresses of any such workshop. This would have seemed to be their great chance to strike out against Julsrud, but no such superartistic family has ever been found in Acambaro even after intensive search. At one time, Julsrud claimed there was an attempt to slip into the collection an obvious fake in an attempt to discredit it.

Professor Hapgood was present when a dig was made in the floor of a house that had been built on the site twenty-five years ago. The Acambaro chief of police lived in the house, and there was no indication that anyone had any chance of hiding anything under the house since about 1930. Forty-three Julsrud-type artifacts were found in this dig, plus miscellaneous other Indian artifacts. Over the five-acre site (now largely covered with squatters' houses), other finds similar to the Julsrud collection were made, both on the surface and underground.

In 1952, Charles C. DiPeso of the Amerind Foundation, Inc., of Arizona gave his impressions on Acambaro.[1] He stopped by the area for one afternoon and the next morning. He watched Tinajero and a helper dig out some objects and claimed he found evidence of fakery. One has the impression all through the article that he was very ready to find such evidence. Others have commented that DiPeso's observations showed him either a "liar or a fool." DiPeso claimed none of the objects gave any indication of having been buried a long time. Yet Professor Hapgood and Ivan T. Sanderson found objects and parts of figurines showing hard incrustations of

---

[1]Charles C. DiPeso, "The Clay Monsters of Acambaro," *Archeology* (Summer 1953).

dirt, rootlet marks, cavities solidly filled with dirt and sand, etc., all of which indicate burial for some considerable period of time.

Professor Hapgood suggests that the digger's habit of covering up partly excavated caches to keep the neighboring children from taking them overnight might have misled DiPeso. Other scientists have watched the actual excavation of objects, among them Dr. Raymond C. Barber, of the Los Angeles County Museum, and Dr. Eduardo Noguera. The former is a mineralogist, but the latter was director of Pre-Hispanic monuments in Mexico. He found no evidence of fraud at the time, but later came out for fraud on the basis of *his* inability to explain the reptile forms related to man!

One rather disreputable and distasteful method of discrediting the Acambaro collection was used by DiPeso. His article in *Archeology* starts out by saying: "Strange stories have been whispered about in the railroad town of Acambaro . . . they concern a haunted hill where it is said the devil has left many odd and terrible clay figurines strewn on the ground as a warning to mortals." While this may be an excellent start for a weird fiction story, it is rather poor for an article pretending to present an unbiased evaluation of a scientific situation. Neither Hapgood nor Sanderson mention any rumors about the devil nor any story about this hill being "haunted." In fact, squatters were beginning to build on the site while the diggings were going on. This suggests that the peasantry of the area weren't very worried about any "hauntings" in the area. DiPeso could only have introduced this "haunted hill" bit as a deliberate attempt to discredit the whole story with no consideration for the truth of the matter.

DiPeso also befogged the issue by saying:"These ceramic figures consist of such forms as Brontosaurus, Tyrannosaurus Rex, Stegosaurus, Trachodon, Dimetrodon, and other Mesozoic reptilian forms . . . ." But Professor Hapgood presented photos of hundreds of the reptile figurines to Dr. A. S. Romer, Professor of Zoology at Harvard University. Professor Romer said they were not typical of any known fossil species of dinosaurs. Romer suggested they might have been inspired by living reptiles of the area. DiPeso apparently does not know a Tyrannosaur when he sees it.

But most importantly, there has recently been an event that strongly indicates that the Julsrud objects are of considerable antiquity. Professor Hapgood obtained parts of one figurine that had organic matter included in it when molded. These were sent to the radiocarbon laboratory of Isotopes, Inc., at Westwood, New Jersey, in September 1968. Back came the amazing result: the organic material was 3590 years old, plus or minus 100 years! This means that the object was either made about 1600 B.C.—or some native Mexican artisan was smart enough to put some old organic material in some of the figurines. This latter seems highly doubtful, since radiocarbon dating was only being developed in the late 1940s, and had hardly become popularized when the purchase of the figurines was halted in 1952.

It might be interesting to note that the C-14 dating of 3600 B.P. or 1600 B.C., falls into that strange time period of 1700 to 1500 B.C. in which so many things happened. Great natural catastrophes struck the Mediterranean; Crete and Egypt fell; in India, the Indus valley civilization came to a sudden end; the volcano of Santorini blew up in Greece; and many legends of these occurrences have come down to us. If the C-14 dating correctly puts the Acambaro figurines in this period, could there by any connection between catastrophes in these other cultures and the strange flowering of the Julsrud culture in Mexico?

In general, the animal figurines are often modeled with an excellent feel for movement, and one can tell usually what they are supposed to be. But the details are rarely specific. For instance, one of the figures is obviously an elephantine figure. It appears to be most similar to the Indian elephant, but none of the details are modeled accurately. If modeled on the Indian elephant, it seems unlikely that an ancient Mexican would have seen one. It was more likely that he might still see a live mammoth, but the figure is not mammoth-like.[2] It is true, however, that in 1931 the city of Acambaro installed a fountain in the town square with a crude statue of an elephant thereon.

---

[2]Ronald J. Willis, "Man and the Mammoth in the Americas," *INFO Journal*, vol. I, no. 1 (1967).

Another aspect of the collection, of which we unfortunately have no good photos, is that of fabulous animals with their parts intermingled in various ways. Also some of the humanoid forms have forked tongues, webbed hands and feet, etc. In short, we have the human imagination run rife.

Mr. Julsrud himself had the theory that the collection was in an Aztec museum in Tenochtitlan, and that it had derived from Atlantis before its destruction. When the Spaniards came to Mexico, the collection supposedly was moved to Acambaro and buried by the Aztecs. The way Tinajero described finding the objects was curious. They seemed to exist in "pockets" of many figurines, all jumbled together. No human graves seemed to be connected with the "pockets" of figurines. However, six human skulls have been found in the area, and these seem to represent great degrees of dolichocephalism (long headedness) and brachycephalism (round headedness), but this is as expected in American Indian populations. Unfortunately these have not been intensively studied to date.

There seems to be no end to the intriguing story of Acambaro. Professor Hapgood was also present at a dig made in the barnyard of Colonel Muzquiz. Previously some digging in this barnyard had turned up Tarascan pottery, and an "enormous skull was found at a considerable depth associated with a large flat stone." It is conceivable that this skull was that of a mammoth, since they abound in the area. Indeed, a mammoth skeleton was found right next to the area from which the Acambaro figurines came, and it was sent to Mexico City. The association of the skull with a flat stone suggests that humans in the area might have had something to do with the skull's deposit.

Professor Hapgood decided to try to reopen this pit where the skull had been found. He noticed that the ground therein was still soft and powdery though it had been refilled four or five years previously. The flat stone wasn't found, but something stranger was—a flight of stairs leading downward! The Colonel remembered that the previous dig had found suggestions of a tunnel going back into the hill. The stairway was filled with what appeared to be hard-packed volcanic material, but unfortunately neither time nor money allowed it to be excavated further. We wonder what was at the end of that stairway and tunnel going into the hill that yielded such strange things almost on its surface!

Professor Hapgood found that a Mr. Ferro in San Miguel Allende was finding many figurines and had sold over 1,500 to visitors to the area at very good prices. He had, in fact, a salesroom in the American art school in the town. He claimed he could tell "real" antiquities from "fake." Over a dozen objects on his shelves were very similar to the Julsrud objects, including part of a mask, a woman standing on a lizard, a giant with a reptile, a woman with a fish tail, and five tableaux. Hapgood and Ferro then visited the site of the finding of this material and found it was *in* the San Miguel Allende pyramids! Holes in twenty of the pyramids showed where Ferro had dug out saleable materials, and here, the figurines were often found in graves themselves, unlike Acambaro. Here, then, was another source of the Julsrud figurines, but most of them are hopelessly dispersed to numerous American collectors. Curiously, because a few fakes were once found being made in the area, the whole group of objects coming from this area also were considered fakes by the archeological authorities. Professor Hapgood considered that the findings at San Miguel Allende tended to give credence to the validity of the Acambaro objects.

It should also be mentioned that strange ceramic figurines are not limited to central Mexico. Nachtigall[3] shows a ceramic lizard-beast from La Plata, Ecuador, that reminds one of some of the fantastic creatures in the Acambaro collection.

To what conclusion can we come then? There is much data to show that the Acambaro figurines may well be of considerable antiquity. Yet it is difficult to accept that there was an Indian culture in ancient Mexico that could have had extensive knowledge of only recently discovered large reptiles and Pleistocene animals and that could have produced objects so similar to many other culture patterns. Perhaps applying some of the recently devised

[3]Horst Nachtigall, *Die Amerikanischen Megalithkulturn*, (Berlin: Dietrich Reimer Verlag, 1958).

tests to the ceramics such as X-ray fluoroscopy or thermoluminescence would help establish the approximate dates of the objects. It is conceivable that some of the collection might be fakes, i.e. less than 100 years old, while others are many thousands. Yet the C-14 test has already given a date of 3600 B.P., which archeologists have, to the author's knowledge, ignored entirely. Would other tests fare any better?

And how about the teeth from the extinct Pleistocene horse, *Equus Conversidens* Owen? How did they get mixed into the collection? The collection does have figurines that seem to represent horses and perhaps Pleistocene horses. Can there be any connection between the teeth and the horse figurines? Did an ancient Mexican Indian extrapolate the horse from its teeth? Or did he see the horse alive? Or is it a subtle piece of fakery?

Sanderson sums up his investigation so: "Either the old gentleman [Julsrud] has made one of the greatest chance discoveries of all time or has been mildly imposed upon for many years by a person or persons who wished nothing more than to earn a modest stipend . . . ." Our conclusion can likewise be only tentative—at worst, we have an amazing collection of art, but if genuinely old, a collection that may revolutionize our view of ancient Mexican culture and history.

The author extends thanks to Professor Charles Hapgood who made available his extensive notes and photos on Acambaro, and likewise to Ivan T. Sanderson who supplied important notes on his site visit. This article would have been impossible without this material. There is very little published on the Acambaro problem.

# THE COSO ARTIFACT
## Ronald J. Willis

*As Louis Pauwels and I indicated in* L'homme éternel, *the Coso object may be a proof of the existence of advanced technological civilizations in the past. From the scientific point of view, therefore, this is probably the most important article in this book.*

On February 13, 1961, Mike Mikesell, Wallace A. Lane, and Virginia Maxey were collecting interesting mineral specimens, particularly geodes, about six miles northeast of Olancha, Calif. They were the owners of the LM & V Rockhounds Gem and Gift Shop in Olancha. Promising specimens that might yield semi-precious stones were often collected and taken back to the shop for investigation.

This day a sack of rocks was picked up near the top of a peak about 4,300 feet in elevation and about 340 feet above the dry bed of Owens Lake. One stone picked up was thought to be a geode at first, although it had an incrustation of fossil shells and their

13

fragments on it. Geologists think that, about 1,000 years ago, the level of Owens Lake came up to the point where the specimen was collected.

Next day back in their shop, Mike Mikesell cut the "geode" in two with a ten-inch diamond saw. The rock was difficult to cut, and later it was found to have completely ruined the new diamond saw blade. There was no cavity in the rock as would be found in many geodes. Instead there was a perfectly circular section of some very hard ceramic or porcelain material, with a two-millimeter shaft of bright metal in the center.

Figure A (see photo insert) shows the two outside halves of the rock after having been sliced in two. In the upper half, the dark material to the left with the shiny spots on it is some sort of tarnished metal.

Figure B (see photo insert) shows the inside of the two halves. Notice the two sides show some evidence of having been surrounded with something which has left a hexagonal cavity.

Though it has been called a "geode" from time to time by its finders and others, it is not a true geode. The outer crust is of hardened clay with pebbles and fossil shell inclusions. In the crust (but not visible in the photos) it is claimed are two allegedly non-magnetic objects resembling a nail and a washer.

It was thought at first that the material filling the hexagonal cavity was petrified wood. It was suggested that the wood had originally been carved out to the hexagonal shape to form some sort of case or covering for the object. It is not clear what the finders think this layer of the "geode" is. Figure 1 gives a schematic drawing of the bottom half of the rock in figure B.

A close inspection of figure B shows that whatever did fill the hexagonal portion of the mass, part of it has been lost in the lower half of the mass. Whatever the material may be, it would appear to be rather soft and crumbly, if part of it fell out when the object was halved.

Figures C and D represent respectively, the lower and upper halves as shown in figure B. These two figures are X-ray photos and mainly show only the metal in the "geode." Clearly some partly

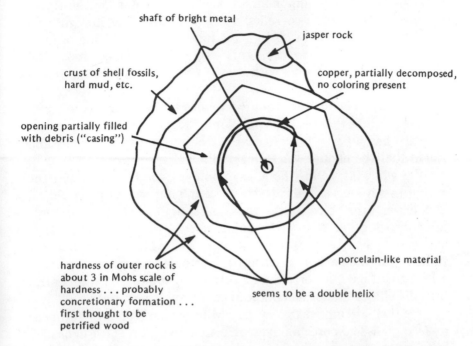

shaft of bright metal

jasper rock

crust of shell fossils,
hard mud, etc.

copper, partially decomposed,
no coloring present

opening partially filled
with debris ("casing")

hardness of outer rock is
about 3 in Mohs scale of
hardness . . . probably
concretionary formation . . .
first thought to be
petrified wood

seems to be a double helix

porcelain-like material

Figure 1. Schematic drawing of the bottom half of the Coso artifact.

metallic object was embedded in the rock and has been cut in two, with about half of it sticking into each half of the rock.

The central object in the rock is a two-millimeter shaft of bright metal. This was cut in two in 1961 but five years afterwards had no tarnishing visible. Surrounding this is about ¾ inches of some ceramic material. And visible around the outside of this seems to be some copper material, which is partially decomposed. The only magnetic part of the object is the central shaft of bright metal, according to the finders.

When looking over this object, the first thing that occurs to one—with the juxtaposition of regular-shaped ceramics, metallic shaft, the remains of copper—is that it is some sort of electrical apparatus. In looking at the X-ray photos, it appears that the shaft goes through all the components shown in the photos, and in figure C, seems to have been corroded at the end. However in figure D, the shaft unmistakenly ends in what appears to be a spring or helix of metal. There are three segments of the object on the shaft, and the central one of ceramics with some corroded copper is the visible one that has been sliced in two.

There is no indication from the photos (the author has not seen the object) that there is any question of fraud. One geologist (not named!) has reportedly looked at the object and its coverings and stated that the nodule was at least 500,000 years old!

But while inspecting the X-ray photos of the Coso artifact, the author asked Paul J. Willis to try to sketch out as best he could an idea of what the object in the rock mass might look like. Suddenly after drawing one sketch, he said, "Say, you know what has a hexagonal part like this—a spark plug!" I was thunderstruck, for suddenly all the parts seemed to fit. The object sliced in two shows a hexagonal part, a porcelain or ceramic insulator, with a central metallic shaft—the basic components of any spark plug.

We then attempted to saw an ordinary spark plug in two near its hexagon. The porcelain was of course too hard for a hacksaw, but the plug came apart and we found all the components similar to the Coso artifact, but with some differences. The copper ring around the halves displayed in the object seems to correspond to a copper sealer ring in the upper part of the steel casing of any spark plug. The hexagonal area in the mass is probably made up of rust, the remains of this steel casing. The lower end of the object seems to be corroded away, so not much can be made of it.

It should also be noted that the central shaft of a spark plug is made of a metal that has a slightly brassy tint, which Mrs. Maxey mentioned as a characteristic of the central shaft of the object.

The upper end of the object seems to end in a spring; however, there is some possibility that what is seen in the X-ray photo is actually the remains of a corroded piece of metal with threads. The larger upper metallic piece in the Coso artifact does not seem to correspond exactly with any part on the everyday spark plug we use now. Figure 2 is an attempt to point out the similarities of the Coso object and a modern spark plug.

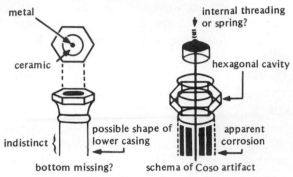

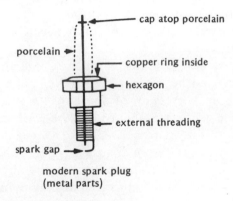

Figure 2. Schematic comparison of the Coso artifact to the modern spark plug.

But if the Coso artifact is actually a spark plug, or something similar, how old is it, where did it come from, and what is it doing encased in something its finders call "rock"? To begin with, it is not really clear what the material surrounding the Coso artifact actually is. In one place, Mrs. Maxey refers to it as "hardened clay" and it does seem to have picked up a miscellaneous collection of pebbles, the "nail and washer," etc., on its surface. If the material is not a sedimentary rock, it is much easier to explain it. It may be an old spark plug from some years ago that has in some manner collected a concretion of mud which has hardened around it. The surface material is noted as having a hardness of Mohs 3, not really very hard. The diamond saw may have had trouble only because the individual using it did not realize that there was something as hard as porcelain in the object, yet one commonly finds quartz crystals in geodes, and quartz is somewhat harder than porcelain. One notes from a geologic map of the area in which the object was found, that there are many old mining shafts and small mines, one of which is less than two miles from the site.

If this object is not a product of our modern technology, it surely represents one of the most important objects ever found. One doesn't imagine the California Indians using spark plugs, although some technological inventions appear early and are lost again, such as the crystal lens of Nineveh and the Babylonian electrical batteries.

Luckily, we were able to call on INFO member Egan who lives in California, and he made a trip to visit Mrs. Maxey and Mr. Lane, who is in possession of the object now. Mrs. Maxey now states that the center metallic rod of the artifact is not magnetic, though she stated in an article in *Desert Magazine* (February 1961), "Only this metal core responds to a magnet." She is of the opinion that it was this metallic piece that made the object so hard to saw through. Mr. Lane has the object on display in his home. He states that the object is for sale for $25,000—a bit stiff if it is really only an old spark plug. It is claimed that several museums are interested in the object, including the Smithsonian, but if the Smithsonian is after it, it must be for the sole purpose of losing it in their cavernous warehouses, for this is what happens to most of their specimens.

There is no indication that any professional scientist has ever carefully examined the object, so what it may be is still questionable. The Coso artifact now seems to join the club with the Casper, Wyoming mummy and other Fortean objects, whose owners refuse to allow anyone to examine the object in question without an exorbitant payment.

Special thanks to INFO member Ronald Calais, who first brought the Coso object to our attention, and who did all the basic research on it.

# THE MIMA MOUNDS

## Elton Caton

*H.P. Lovecraft and other writers of fantastic tales have created the legend of the artificial American mounds considered as entrances to an unknown world. We have no desire to write fiction— but it is nevertheless interesting to note that similar mounds exist in Russia, Mongolia, and China.*

*Are they a widespread, natural phenomenon? Or are they the traces of a civilization that once covered the entire world?*

*The future will tell us.*

Near the southern tip of Puget Sound there are hundreds of acres of strange mounds. Scientists have proposed several explanations:

*a*) built by ancient men
*b*) made by giant fish during a period when the prairies were submerged by water
*c*) enormous anthills
*d*) gophers

If you look from a good vantage point at the edge of one of the prairies, you will see thousands of mounds, all beautifully symmetrical, rising up out of the ground like huge globes, half-buried in the earth.

In some areas there are as many as 10,000 of these mounds within a square mile. The biggest ones are seven or eight feet high, and the smallest are barely discernable bumps. They may be anywhere from six to seventy feet in diameter. The bigger they are, the more symmetrical they seem to be. The mounds in any one area are approximately the same height.

The mounds have been a source of puzzlement since the United States Exploring Expedition, under the command of Commander Charles Wilkes, sailed into Puget Sound in 1841. Thinking they were ancient burial mounds, he set about having one of them excavated. Not a single bone was found. He then had two others excavated but found no bones.

Since then, hundreds of mounds have been opened, but no one has found the smallest relic to suggest that human beings had the slightest hand in their building. The prairie on which the most impressive examples of the mounds are found is called the Mima Prairie (hence the Mima Mounds). The word Mima is from the Chinook language, and its meaning is related to the idea of death and burial. However, there are no known Indian legends to explain the mounds.

One of the least credible explanations for the mounds was expounded by an eminent scientist, Louis Agassiz. He looked at a sketch of the mounds and heard them described. Promptly, he announced that they were the nests of fish (a species of sucker) built at a time when the prairies were covered by water. Other absurdities aside, the Washington prairies were never covered by fresh water, and they were only under postglacial seawater for a short time.

At one time, an ant theory had quite a play. A large black ant, called *Formica sanguinea*, lives in the sparse stands of evergreens near the prairies. The nests that it builds are made of pine needles and bits of twigs, but they are sometimes five feet high. It is not too hard to imagine some ancient breed of ants building even higher mounds of gravel and silt. This theory collapsed when some good-sized pebbles and stones were found inside a number of the Mima mounds.

Over the years, a number of geological clues have been discovered. Nobody agrees just where the clues point, but at least they have to be reckoned with. Some of the findings are described by J. Harlan Bretz, for a Washington Geological Survey bulletin.

Well-developed mounds are found only on the outwash plains of the Vashon Glacier, which covered the area some 15,000 years ago.

The mounds are set close together, but there is no pattern to their arrangement.

The same sort of pebbly gravel and black silt mixture that makes up the mounds also covers the prairies between the mounds. However, between the mounds, the mixture is only a few inches deep; in the mounds, it reaches from top to bottom.

Boulders are scattered around some of the mound prairies; when you look at the base of the mounds, you will see this same scattering effect. So it seems that the boulders were there first.

Under the silt mixture that makes up the prairie's top layer, there is a gravel base that extends to an undetermined depth. Some of the mounds have "arms" of black silt, about a foot long, which extend down into the gravel base. Not all mounds have those "roots," only some of them do.

There is another theory that has been advanced by Arthur M. Ritchie, formerly a geologist for the Washington State Highway Department. Ritchie feels that the mounds' formation began when the ice had retreated, but while the ground was still frozen. Subsequent thawing and freezing cracked the mud into a number of polygonal shapes, not an unusual pattern to find in various parts of the world today.

On the mound prairies, ice formed in the cracks. As the ice built up, more soil was shoved into the polygon of earth, and the cracks themselves widened. Finally the earth blocks froze too. When a big thaw set in, the ice in the cracks flowed away, leaving big polygons of earth standing (thawing more slowly than the ice). The rounded shapes are accounted for by erosion.

Other scientists have picked out flaws in Ritchie's theory. They question if the area had the sort of climate that Ritchie describes. They argue that the region was not much colder during the mound-forming time than it is today.

There is also the gopher theory. This theory was first advanced by Walter W. Dalquist in 1941 when he was making a survey of the mammals of southern Washington. He later developed the theory with Victor Sheffer, a biologist with the U.S. Fish and Wildlife Service.

They point out that wherever the mounds occur there are (or have been) gophers. They postulate that as the Vashon ice sheet retreated and as vegetation grew up in its wake, pocket gophers began moving in from the south. Finally, at the southern end of Puget Sound, they ran into a young evergreen forest that had grown up as the glacier retreated.

Gophers will not live in the shade of a forest, so instead of pushing on farther, they dug in on the prairies.

They say (Dalquist and Sheffer) that each mound represents the "territory" of a gopher family and that the mound was a series of foraging tunnels; the "mound roots" were also abandoned tunnels that filled up with silt.

Opponents of this theory point out that not all of the mounds have the silt "roots." Also, one geologist wrote: "After diligent search, more than fifty stones have been taken from inside the mounds. The stones range in size from two to twenty inches in diameter and many of them were found well above the base of the mound."

The question has been asked, "How could a gopher shove a stone the size of a football up to the top of his nest?"

To top it all off, there are those who say that the mounds are growing. Over thirty years ago, farmers in the area started talking about it.

Doctor Sheffer, for one, takes this seriously.

*Reference*

Muir, Jean. 1968. "The Mystery of the Mima Mounds." *True*, January issue: 56, 72–73.

# THE MYSTERIOUS MOONSHAFT
## Antonin T. Horak

*If the "Prague spring" had continued, and if trips to Czecho-slovakia had not become difficult and even dangerous, I would have done some on-the-spot research into this story.*

*This is the story of the discovery in October 1944, during the Czech resistance against the German invaders, of a cave in the form of a crescent-shaped shaft, seemingly of artificial origin. Czech friends have confirmed the basic facts of this story, which was made public in March 1965. Unfortunately they have other problems at this moment, and I can understand their position.*

*The riddle is as strange as it is fascinating. The work of extraterrestrial beings is the first explanation that comes to mind, and is the one I would prefer.*

*I hope that more detailed research using modern methods will one day bring us the truth about a mystery that is one of the most astonishing in this book and on this planet.*

The following true adventure, related by a captain in the Slovak

Uprising of World War II, transpired during October of 1944. Dr. Antonin T. Horak—now a linguist—has attempted for years to persuade speleologists to investigate what he considers one of the underworld's strangest mysteries—an ancient shaft he discovered in a dismal Czechoslovakian cave. The story is taken from a diary written on the scene and is reprinted from the March, 1965, issue of NSS NEWS (National Speleological Society) by permission of the author. The cave in question is located near the villages of Plavince and Lubocna, at about 49.2 degrees north, 20.7 degrees east— Ronald Calais [contributor of the diary].

*October 23, 1944.* Early yesterday, Sunday, October 22nd, Slavek found us in a trench and hid us in this grotto. Today at nightfall, he and his daughter Hanka came with food and medicine. We had not eaten since Friday, and all we had had before, during the last two battles, was maize bread and not enough of that. Our commissary had been on its last legs anyway; the supply carriers had been dispersed by confusion and the enemy.

Saturday afternoon, the remnants of our battalion (184 men and officers, a quarter wounded, 16 stretcher cases) were retreating through the snow of the north slope. My company was the rear guard. At dawn Sunday, two 70mm. guns opened-up at us from close range—about 300 meters. Having held our position for 12 hours, I ordered a gradual breakup of the skirmish and a slip-off. But in our left trench, someone became careless, and that drew two direct hits—shells, two wounded. Arriving there, I bumped into the enemy, caught a bayonet and bullet with my left palm and a blow on the head, which put me out. Without my fur cap, it might have been fractured.

I came to when someone was pulling me from the trench, a tall peasant. He packed snow on my hand and head, and grinned. Then this rough and ready Samaritan grabbed Jurek, stripped off his pants, yanked a long sliver of steel from his thigh, and planted him bare-bottomed and gasping into a heap of snow. Martin, with a slash across and into his belly, was tenderly bandaged. Building a stretcher, the peasant introduced himself as Slavek, a sheepman, owner of the pastures hereabouts. With Slavek hauling and guiding, it took us four hours to reach this cranny.

Slavek moved rocks in the cranny and opened a low cleft, the entrance to this roomy grotto. Placing Martin in a niche, we were astonished to see Slavek become ceremonious: he crossed himself, each of us, the grotto, and, with a deep bow, its back wall, where a hole came to my attention.

About to leave us, Slavek went through the same holy rites, and begged me not to go further into his cave. I accompanied him to fetch pine boughs, and he told me that only once, with his father and grandfather, had he been in this cave; that it was a huge maze, full of pits which they never wanted to fathom, pockets of poisonous air, and "certainly haunted." I was back in the grotto with my men at about midnight, exhausted, head very painful, soothed it with snow. Martin was unconscious, Jurek feverish. For breakfast-lunch-dinner, he and I had hot water, and, thank God, I had my pipe. I placed warm stones around Martin, and Jurek got the first watch.

Miserable night. Martin at times conscious; I gave him three aspirins and hot water to sip with drops of Slivovitz [Eds. Note: brandy]. Jurek hobbled hungrily around the two German helmets in which he boiled water to which I added ten drops of Slivovitz, our breakfast. With this deluge of snow, avalanches imminent, and enemy skiers roaming, Slavek may not be able to get through to us with food for days to come. And neither should I try hunting and track up the landscape while I have two immobilized men on my hands. But here we have this cave which Slavek knows only partially; it may have more than this known entrance, and it may contain hibernating animals. These possibilities I mulled over while Jurek was chewing pine bark, and, as expected, he implored me to go poaching into Slavek's cave and promised to keep mum. And I was not only starved but equally eager to find out what makes self-assured Slavek scared enough to invoke the deities. I started my cave tour with rifle, lantern, torches, pick. After a not too devious nor dangerous walk and some squeezings, always taking the easiest and marking side passages, I came, after about 1½ hours, into a long, level passage, and at its end upon a barrel-sized hole.

Crawling through and still kneeling, I froze in amazement—there stands something like a large, black silo, framed in white. Regaining breath, I thought that this is a bizarre, natural wall or curtain of black salt, or ice, or lava. But I became perplexed, then awestruck, when I saw that it is a glass-smooth flank of a seemingly man-made structure which reaches into the rocks on all sides. Beautifully, cylindrically curved it indicates a huge body with a diameter of about 25 meters. Where this structure and the rocks meet, large stalagmites and stalactites form that glittering white frame. The wall is uniformly blue-blackish, its material seems to combine properties of steel, flint, rubber—the pick made no marks and bounced off vigorously. Even the thought of a tower-sized artifact, embedded in rock in the middle of an obscure mountain, in a wild region where not even legend knows about ruins, mining, industry, overgrown with age-old cave deposits, is bewildering—the fact is appalling.

Not immediately discernible, a crack in the wall appears from below, about 20 to 25 cm. wide, tapers off and disappears into the cave's ceiling, 2 to 5 cm. wide. Its insides, right and left, are pitch black and have fist-sized, sharp valleys and crests. The crack's bottom is a rather smooth trough of yellow sandstone, and drops very steeply (about 60 degrees) into the wall. I threw a lighted torch through; it fell and extinguished with loud cracklings and hissings as if a white hot ploughshare were dropped into a bucket.

Driven to explore, and believing myself thin enough to get through this upside-down keyhole, I went in. Wriggling sideways, injured hand and head below and steeply downward, nearly standing on my head, cramped, though my right arm with the lamp could move in the extended crack above me, the crush got the better of me and I had to get out, back, quickly. And that became a struggle. When out and breath regained, I was too fascinated by the whole riddle and determined to get at it. For the day I had had enough and had to think about tactics.

I was in camp about 4:00 P.M. Jurek had washed Martin, kept

him between warm stones, and I gave him three aspirins and hot water with Slivovitz to sip. I explained to Jurek that the hunt in the cave requires much smoke, poles, and a rope. Thank God, Slavek and Hanka did come with provisions. When they left, I accompanied them to fetch torch boughs, was back in camp about 2:00 A.M., dead tired, but finally we had eaten—Jurek too much—and I got the second watch.

*October 24, 1944.* Peaceful night; Martin sipped fever-tea with honey; hope we can pull him through. Jurek's posterior is not even swollen, but my head still is. I cut our belts, braided eight meters of solid rope. At 10:00 A.M. was at the wall, anchored the rope over a stick across the crack, and keeping it slung over my shoulder, forced myself again into the grim maw. Like yesterday, the lamp, this time carbide, was on a stick ahead within the jaw above. When it came through and down, it swung freely over some void into which I could not see, and there was again rushing as if from agitated waters. And, unable to turn, I feared a water-filled pit ahead and to end in it—literally—in a headstand.

I wriggled upward, back again; my clothes caught on the protrusions, descended on my shoulders and head, and formed a plug. The resulting struggle nearly caused me to be burned alive. When out and on my feet, I was shaking from exhaustion, and had lurid visions.

There were no loose stones about the wall, and so I hacked stalagmites into short rolls and bowled them down through the crack. They rolled on, causing enormous echoes, and knocked to a standstill, indicating a solid floor and room to turn. I launched the unlit torches after the stones, undressed, keeping the shirt only, and went after the stones and torches. Already acquainted with the meanest fangs in the crack, I came through with only a few cuts, dropped a little, rolled down an incline and was stopped by a wall which felt familiar, satiny smooth like the front wall.

My lamp was still burning next to me, but there were confusing sounds. Lighting some torches, I saw that I was in a spacious, curved, black shaft formed by cliff-like walls which intersect and form a crescent-shaped, nearly vertical tunnel, rather, shaft. I cannot describe the somberness and the endless whisperings, rustlings, and roaring sounds, abnormal echoes from my breathing and movements. The floor is the incline over which I rolled in, a solid lime "pavement."

All the lights together did not reach the ceiling or where these walls end or meet. The horizontal distance between the apexes of the concave backside of the front wall and the convex back wall is about eight meters; along the curve of the back wall is about 25 meters. To explore further I needed more light and my pick, which does not fit through the crack and must be taken apart.

I left jubilant, in a sort of enchantment mixed with determination to explore this large structure, which I believe is unique, singular.

This time with my head up, with no clothes to ensnare and burn me, I was through the crack fairly unscathed, dressed, smoked a pipe, and was underway to my men. I tried to catch some bats, but caught none. Jurek was boiling potatoes and mutton and therefore inclined to excuse my bad huntsmanship; he even appreciated its hardships when he had to grease the scratches on my back and mend my shirt.

Martin had a crumb of bread with honeyed fever-tea. After 6:00 P.M., I went for a new load of torches, was back at about 10:00 P.M. Jurek got both watches.

*October 25, 1944.* We had a good night. Martin seems to mend. Am glad that Jurek's thigh is not yet well enough for him to want to go with me poaching for bats. It is better that he knows nothing about the cave's secret.

I went directly to the wall, undressed like yesterday, smeared mutton fat over me, slid my things through the crack, and went in, feet first. Extending the carbide lamp upon a double pole, with four torches burning, still the upper ends of the cliffs remained in the dark. I fired two bullets up, parallel to the walls. The reports caused roars as from an express train, but no impact was visible. Then I fired a bullet on each wall, aiming some 15 meters upward from me, got large blue-green sparks and such a sound that I had to hold my ears between my knees, and flames danced wildly.

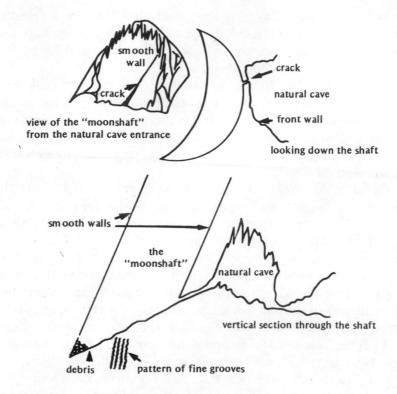

Figure 3. Schematic representation of the mysterious moonshaft.

Assembling the pick caused more uproars. I probed the "pavement," and started digging where the lime is thin, in the horns of the crescent. At right is dry loam; at left I came, at about half a meter, upon a pocket of enamel from the teeth of some large animal; took one canine and one molar, replaced the rest. Digging on nearby, the back wall has, at about 1½ meters below the pavement, a vertical, finely fluted, undulating pattern [R.C.: this has been suggested as an indication of machinery]. It seemed warmer than the smooth surface. I tried with lip and ear, and believe the impression is correct. In the middle, the pavement is too thick for a trenchpick.

When the torches were extinguished, and I was in a freezing sweat, I left the "moonshaft," dressed and went where the bats are, and bagged seven. Jurek stuffed them with bread and herbs and they became exquisite "pigeons."

Slavek and Olga, his other daughter, came about dusk with hay, straw, a sheep's fleece, more medicinal herbs—self-heal and stonecrop—and seeds from the Iris, an excellent coffee substitute. I accompanied him, fetched pine torches, two long poles, and was back about midnight. Martin got the last aspirins, honey-water; and Jurek both watches.

*October 26, 1944.* It was a good night. I went into the "moonshaft" to continue experimenting. On my longest assembly of poles the carbide lamp did not light the upper ends of these cliffs. I fired above the lighted areas; the bullets struck huge sparks and made deafening echoes. Then horizontally at the back wall with similar effects—sparks, roaring, no splinters, but a half-finger-long welt which gave a pungent smell. After that I continued in my digging in the left moon horn and saw that the wavy pattern extends downward; but in the right horn, I found no such pattern.

I left the "moonshaft" to probe the front wall and its surroundings. Next to the stalactites are some enamel-like flecks which, scraped, yield a powder too fine to be collected without glue, which I will try to boil from our "pigeons' " claws. I wished to obtain a sample of the peculiar material of the walls, but even firing two bullets into the crack, upon the protrusions and hitting them, I received only richochets, a blast of thunder, welts, and the same pungent smell.

Returning to camp I caught some bats and we again had "pigeons." I ordered Jurek to carefully remove any trace of them, and kept the claws. The Slaveks arrived as usual at nightfall bringing this time a quarter of a deer, ½ kilogram of salt, and a tin of carbide. Jurek took both watches.

*October 27, 1944.* Martin died, slept into death. Jurek knows his kin, took charge of his belongings, including his wallet with 643 crowns, watch with chain, and my certificate. Now we are free and ready to leave and rejoin our battalion which is somewhere east of

Kosice. With his stick Jurek can march some ten kilometers daily, and we have to move carefully anyway. We will start tomorrow.

At 10:00 A.M. I was in the cave probing passages for a way around behind the "moonshaft"; looked also for ice and poisonous air about which Slavek had spoken, and found none, though there may be some. Then I slipped into the "moonshaft" to sketch, dig, and ponder, and returned to camp at about 4:00 P.M. I ordered Jurek to prepare our packs, clean the weapons, boil food for seven days, and have ready what we will not need to be returned to the Slaveks. He and both girls, as if the family had sensed that Martin died, came, and we carried him into the dwarf pines to the trench where he had received his mortal wound, took turns to dig his grave, prayed, and buried him in a blanket.

*October 28, 1944.* Restful night, good breakfast. Cut my name, etc., on a leather strip, and together with the golden back of my watch rolled and inserted both engravings into a glass bottle, plugged it with a pebble and a ball of clay mixed with charcoal, and deposited this record in the "moonshaft" on top of the ashes of my torches. It may stay there for a long time, possibly until the structure is completely hidden behind its curtain of stalactites and stalagmites. Slavek has no son to tell about his cave-mystery; his womenfolk don't know about it, and anyway daughters usually marry to other villages. In a few decades nobody will know, if I do not come back and have the structure explored.

I sat there by my fire speculating: What is this structure, with walls two meters thick and a shape that I cannot imagine of any purpose known nowadays? How far does it reach into the rocks? Is there more behind the "moonshaft"? Which incident or who put it into this mountain? Is it a fossilized man-made object? Is there truth in legends, like Plato's, about long lost civilizations with magic technologies which our rationale cannot grasp nor believe?

I am a sober, academically trained person but must admit that there, between those black, satiny, mathematically-curved cliffs I do feel as if in the grip of an exceedingly strange and grim power. I can understand that simple but intelligent and practical men like Slavek and his forebears sense here witchery, conceal it, and also fear that if the existence of this "moonshaft" is ever made known, it would attract armies of tourists, and all the commotion, tunneling and blasting, hotels, and commercialization which would probably ruin their nature-bound trade and honest life.

On my way back to camp I burrowed and hid the crawl holes which lead towards the wall; the cave may have entrances which Slavek does not know, and some chance discoverer may start blasting "for treasure" before a scientific team can get there. I was in camp after 3:00 P.M., and about 5:00 all three Slaveks arrived, bringing some hard-boiled eggs.

With the hearty Slovak handshakes, we shouldered our weapons and packs and went. When we entered the pines and turned, we saw Slavek concealing his cave and the girls sweeping away our tracks. The moon was bright and the snow glittered.

In the very last days of World War II, on my way towards Bohemia, I revisited the place. The Slaveks lived temporarily at Zdar. I visited Martin's grave and looked at the cave entrance. I had taken the animal teeth I had collected to the curator of paleontology at Uzhorod, and he classified them as adult cave bear, *Ursus spaeleus*. Thereupon I speculated: the crack is too small; the lump of limestone and stalagmites in front of the crack would not let any debris through; this bear seems to have fallen into the "moonshaft," which may have had a connection to the surface.

On my last visit to the place, I examined the mountainside above the cave and found no sinkholes or pits, the assumed connections toward the "moonshaft." But on these steep slopes in the Tatra Mountains, rockslides could have obliterated or filled in any such connections.

# THE MYSTERIOUS CEMENT CYLINDERS OF NEW CALEDONIA

## Andrew E. Rothovius

*The discovery in New Caledonia of objects that seem neither natural nor human in origin, or which at least have no relationship to any of the well-known events comprising the human occupation of New Caledonia, is of considerable interest.*

*Supporters of the ancient continent of Mu will of course say that these are remains of Mu. The author of this article (to whom we owe a very interesting study on H. P. Lovecraft and the megaliths of New England) compares these objects with the pillars found in the Marianas Islands. However, there is no proof that the continent of Mu existed. The "interplanetary" hypothesis put forth by the author is equally plausible and probably also equally far from the truth. In this domain, as in others, the truth is probably stranger than fiction, and is at the present time beyond the scope of our imagination. The past is very different from the rigid structures we find in the history books.*

One of the most intriguing and baffling mysteries to confront

35

archaeologists in recent years has been the discovery, in the Southwest Pacific island of New Caledonia and the adjoining Isle of Pines, of some remarkable lime-mortar cylinders that do not appear to be of natural origin, and whose indicated age is far earlier than all previously known man-made cements.

Discovered by L. Chevalier of the Museum of New Caledonia in the island's capital, Noumea, these cylinders run from 40 to 75 inches in diameter, and from 40 to 100 inches in height. They are of a very hard, homogeneous lime-mortar, containing bits of shells, which yield a radiocarbon dating of from 5,120 to 10,950 B.C.— even the lowest date being some 3,000 years earlier than man is believed to have reached the Southwest Pacific from the area of Indonesia. (Lime-mortars of the ancient Mediterranean civilizations do not date earlier than a few hundred years B.C. at the most.)

On their outside, the cylinders are speckled with silica and iron gravel fragments that seem to have hardened into the mortar as it set. This feature is of interest in connection with the tumuli or sand-and-gravel mounds in which the cylinders were found, and that are as peculiar as the cylinders themselves.

There exist 400 of these tumuli on the Isle of Pines, and 17 so far located on New Caledonia itself, at a locality called Païta. On the Isle of Pines, the tumuli consist of a gravelly sand with high iron oxide content; the Païta tumuli are of a siliceous sand. In both places, the tumuli are from 8 to 9 feet high, and average 300 feet in diameter—bare and featureless, with little or no vegetation taking root in the sands of which they are composed.

To date, only four of the tumuli have been excavated. No bones, artifacts, or charcoal were found despite a thorough search; yet three of the tumuli contained one cylinder each, and the fourth had two of them, side by side. In each case, the cylinders were positioned in the center of the tumuli (which appear to resemble giant ant heaps), set vertically.

The impression that M. Chevalier had was that the mortar had been poured into narrow pits dug into the tops of the tumuli and allowed to harden in position. Bits of the sand and gravel composing the tumuli would naturally have worked into the mortar, thereby explaining their presence in the outer surfaces of the cylinders.

But what conceivable reason could there be for their being cast at all, in the first place? Natural origin appears ruled out—yet no evidence has been found of any human association with them, or with the tumuli, which are also inexplicable as natural phenomena.

One might speculate that perhaps some vehicle from another realm than our Earth had hovered overhead . . . and had sent down several hundred investigators in small separate craft, somewhat akin to the LEM module in our Apollo moon-landing craft. When these scouts needed to return to the mother craft, they required small launching pedestals, for which they mixed and poured the lime-mortar into the tops of the sand-and-gravel tumuli they heaped up for this purpose. . . .

Fanciful? Admittedly, yes; for what kind of launching mechanism can it have been that left no visible traces on the cylinder tops? Yet, unless some imaginative solution is sought to the mystery they present, the chances are that science will ignore the New Caledonia tumuli and cement cylinders, when it finds no orthodox explanation for them . . . and they will run the risk of being destroyed and forgotten, when an airport or other major project comes into the area. (New Caledonia was a highly important staging base for the American forces in World War II, and its strategic location makes it highly likely that additional airport developments, whether civilian or military, can be expected there in the not too distant future.)

A possible parallel to the New Caledonia cylinders may perhaps be cited in the strange capped stone pillars on Tinian Island in the Marianas, several thousand miles northwest of New Caledonia. In April, 1819, the French exploring expedition under Captain Louis-Claude de Freycinet in the frigate *Uranie*, visited on Tinian a peculiar spot where, in the midst of lush vegetation on every hand, only a meager growth of grass could be found surrounding a double row of stone pillars, about 15 feet high, each topped by a hemispherically shaped boulder, the rounded side resting on the pillar. While the pillars were still in a good state of preservation, their squared sides and corners only slightly eroded, the boulders were more or less crumbling away; being possibly of a softer stone, though M. de Freycinet's account does not make this point clear.

The French explorers did speculate on whether the pillars had once supported a roof or platform, but they could find no trace of any. What puzzled them most was the aridity and sparseness of the grass around the pillars, though the soil as far as they could determine was just as fertile as that from which the rampant jungle sprouted only a few feet away.

Tinian was successively under Spanish, German, and Japanese occupation until the U.S. Marine landing in 1944—and none of these administrations encouraged foreign scientific research. In any event, no further account of the strange stone pillars has been located by this writer, and it is possible that if they still survived in 1944, they were destroyed in the intense fighting that followed the American landing, before the island was secured as the base from which the B-29s made their devastating strikes against the Japanese homeland.

## References

Freycinet, Louis-Claude de. 1825. *Voyage autour du Monde plus Atlas Historique.* Paris. Pp. 279-80.

*Radiocarbon.* June 1966. Vol. 8. New Haven: Yale University Press. Report on C-14 datings by the Centre des Faibles Radioactivités, C.N.R.S., Gif-sur-Yvette, Essonnes, France.

*Revue de la Société d'Etudes Mélanésiennes.* 1964. Noumea. Pp. 24-25.

# PART TWO

## EXTRATERRESTRIAL
## BEINGS AMONG US

# JOHN WINTHROP & UFOS IN COLONIAL NEW ENGLAND

## Andrew E. Rothovius

With all the recent disinterring of old accounts of phenomena similar to the UFO sightings of our present age, it is rather remarkable that—as far as the writer is aware, and he has a fairly wide acquaintance with all the extant UFO literature—no mention has yet been made of the remarkable UFO sightings recorded by Governor John Winthrop in his journal of the first generation of Puritan settlement at Boston in the seventeenth century.

Winthrop's accounts are clear, detailed, and unemotional. There can be no question of their being honest attempts to leave a description of events of whose reality he had no doubt. They are therefore of very great significance to anyone seeking authentic testimony of UFO phenomena during the period of the settlement and colonization of America.

The first of Winthrop's UFO cases occurred in the month of March 1639, only nine years after the Puritan settlement of Boston. James Everell, well known as a "sober, discreet man," and member of the First Church since 1634, was crossing Muddy River—then a sizable inlet of the Charles, in what is now the Back Bay section of filled land in Boston—with two other men in a scow, about ten o'clock at night, when suddenly a great light flared up in the sky above them. This light at first hung stationary, and seemed square or even oblong in shape, about nine feet across, as nearly as Everell could judge.

Abruptly, the light moved swiftly across the Charles toward Charlestown, then came back again. For between two and three hours, it played a continual game of zigzag over the Muddy and Charles rivers, darting away, zooming back, standing still briefly, then resuming the performance. Petrified with fright, Everell and his companions cowered in the bottom of their scow, unable to row or punt. The antics of the darting light seemed to them to resemble the movements of a pig trying to escape capture by running hither and yon.

When it finally disappeared, Everell discovered to his astonishment that although the tide had been running out during all this while, the scow was actually further upstream than when they first sighted the light. Apparently some influence from it had been pushing the scow against the tide. No further description is given by Winthrop of this sighting, other than the statement that the light was seen by "divers other persons afterward, at about the same place."

Five years later, an even more interesting UFO event occurred. On the evening of January 18, 1644, a light about the size of the full moon was seen rising over the northeastern sea horizon, about 8:00 P.M., by many persons on the Boston waterfront. Within a few minutes, another very similar light was noted coming from the east, and approaching the first one, which was now over Noddle's Island in Boston harbor. Now commenced a game of aerial tag between these two lights: "one would close in on the other, then part and close in again divers times, and so until finally they dipped behind the hill in the island, and vanished." At intervals they shot out little flames or sparkles of light, while chasing each other.

At the same time, several persons who were on the water between Boston and Dorchester, claimed they heard a voice out of

the sky enunciating "in a most dreadful manner," the words "boy
. . . boy . . . come away . . . come away." These persons, known to
all as "sober and godly," insisted they heard this summons
repeated about twenty times, from varying directions. Though they
were unable to judge how far away the voice was coming from, it
nevertheless seemed to them "a great distance."

A week later, the lights were seen again; and another seven days
later, the unearthly voice repeated its summons, this time on the
other side of the harbor, over toward Noddle's Island. Winthrop's
only written comment on these events, beyond the bare recording of
them, was that the latter location was near where Captain Chaddock's pinnace had been destroyed a few weeks previously by a
gunpowder explosion in its hold. Chaddock, he states, was said to
be skilled necromantically, and to "have done strange things on the
way from Virginia," where he was under suspicion of having
murdered his master. The bodies of his crewmen killed in the
explosion had all been washed ashore, but Chaddock's body was
never found.

The implication that Winthrop wanted to convey, apparently,
was that the Evil One had come to claim his own in the person of
Chaddock, and that the lights had been attendant imps from Hell.

I have not found any other descriptions of UFO phenomena in
various Colonial writers and diarists besides Winthrop that I have
examined; but in C. C. Lord's *Life and Times in Hopkinton, N.H.*,
1890, there appears an interesting story of UFO-like sightings on
Putney Hill, also known as Gould Hill, in the northern part of town
facing the valley of the Contoocook. A patch of pine forest on the
north side of this hill was said to have been an "Indian lookout"
where redskin sentinels kept watch for enemy marauders. Beginning some time between 1750 and 1800, glowing, slowly moving
balls floating in the air were often sighted over and near this pine
forest—both by day and by night, but most often in the evenings.
Around 1820, a young man, who half a century later told Mr. Lord
of his experience, was followed home for almost two miles by several
of these glowing balls, in the gathering dusk. They would stop
whenever he himself stopped to look back at them, then resume

their movement as soon as he started walking again; but they never came any closer than within fifty feet or so.

Neither in this case, nor in any other one, was there any indication of hostility on the part of the globes, nor was anyone ever harmed by them. By the time that Mr. Lord wrote his history, in the late nineteenth century, they had no longer been seen for at least a generation, but many still recalled them. Curiosity and interest, rather than alarm, seems to have been the chief reaction of those who sighted the Putney Hill globes.

# MYSTERIES OF THE AIRSHIP AGE

## Lyle Gaulding

*Rumors of phantom dirigibles and bizarre aerial machines were rampant throughout Europe and the United States between 1890 and 1914, inspiring such science-fiction books as Jules Verne's* Robur le Conquérant *and Maurice Renard's* Le Péril bleu. *In England, around 1910, reports of zeppelins flying overhead increased to such a point that diplomatic protests were made to Germany. The German emperor personally ordered an investigation, which proved that no zeppelin had left its hangar to fly over England. The mystery has never been solved.*

Mysteries—disappearances and unexplained accidents—concerning ships and airplanes have been fairly well documented and the more notable adequately reported to those interested in books like those of Charles Fort, Vincent Gaddis, and Harold T. Wilkins. But the "Great Age of Airships," roughly from 1900 to 1937, also produced some intriguing and inexplicable cases involving the great lighter-than-air vessels now virtually gone from the world.

A few odd cases worth noting cropped up prior to World War I, some during the "Balloon Era." There were cases of disappearing balloons, and one early case of a balloon that refused to disappear. It was seen repeatedly aloft after being in the Mediterranean. Two of the escape balloons launched from Paris during the siege of 1870 failed to land in Europe. One was seen blowing west over Britain. There can be little doubt that both lost balloons came down at sea, but it remains a puzzle why the pilots did not try to land.

Harold Wilkins, in *Strange Mysteries of Time and Space*, tells of a British member of Parliament, Walter Powell, who was accidentally carried up by a balloon from Bridgeport, Dorset, in 1881. Though an extensive search was carried out, no trace of Powell or the balloon was ever found. This case is particularly notable in that shortly after the disappearance a number of "UFOs" were sighted.

In 1897 the "Great Airship Flap" occurred. An unidentified flying object, or objects, was sighted all over the United States. (And elsewhere? So far as I know, the 1897 "flap" was solely an American phenomenon, but I'd welcome any information to the contrary.) It can hardly be imagined that the 1897 phenomenon was actually a true LTA ship, though the "cow-stealing UFO" reported by A. Hamilton of LeRoy, Kansas, on April 21, 1897, sounds remarkably like a dirigible. Hamilton's experience is mentioned both in Jacques Vallee's *Anatomy of a Phenomenon*, and in Frank Edwards's *Flying Saucers—Serious Business*.

Perhaps the most amusing story to come from the 1897 sightings was reported in the *Dallas Morning News* for April 19, 1897. The story stated that on the morning of the 17th the "Airship" was seen over Aurora, Texas. It passed over the town, struck "Judge Procter's windmill," and exploded. In a deadpan manner, the story continues, saying that the pilot's body had been too mutilated to be described, but was obviously nonhuman. It is also stated that papers bearing unknown symbols were found and that a U.S. Signal Service officer believed that the pilot was from Mars. "The pilot's funeral will take place at noon tomorrow." It may be worth noting that "airship" sightings, including Hamilton's, occurred after the 17th.

Another, and more solemn, air mystery of 1897 was the disappearance of August Andree's balloon expedition to the North Pole. This mystery was solved in 1930 when the remains of the expedition were found on White Island in the Arctic.

Dirigible airships were used in war for the first time in World War I. The most impressive of the ships of war were the giant German Zeppelin. The Zeppelin's most important military service was naval scouting, but the big rigids achieved their greatest notoriety by staging the first large bombing raids against civilian targets. The first raid was carried out against Antwerp by a single Zeppelin late in 1914.

By 1917, improvements in antiaircraft weapons had made the air over Allied cities, especially London, almost impossibly dangerous for the hydrogen-filled airships. However, in October 1917, the German navy decided on a last major effort. On October 19, eleven giant airships, each some 700 feet long, and filled with about 2.3 million cubic feet of hydrogen, met over the English coast at dusk. A cloud layer protected the Zeppelins. For five hours, the grey bombers cruised over the Midlands inflicting considerable damage. Then, about midnight, a storm blew up driving the ships across the Channel. They soon came under attack and were forced up to 20,000 feet where the crews suffered terribly from cold and lack of oxygen. By dawn, six ships had made their way back to Germany, but five were still adrift over France. Soon two were shot down in flames, and the captains of two other ships, unable to maintain high altitude, decided to sacrifice their ships making a forced landing in enemy territory.

Now only one of the five was still in the air. The L-50 was trying to fly back to its home base at high altitude. Over the French Alps the supply of oxygen began to run out and the captain ordered a descent. Soon mountains loomed through the clouds and the captain ordered engines stopped. But the engine crewmen were too weak to respond to orders. The L-50 crashed, the control car and the aft engine gondola being torn off by the alpine peak. As they struggled out of the wreckage, the captain and crew saw the L-50, its gas cells apparently still intact, rise rapidly into the sky and vanish from sight with some (four, by one account) crewmen still aboard. It was never seen again.

What did happen to the derelict Zeppelin? Certainly, it did not come down in Europe. A 700-foot airship in one's cabbage patch, or in the French Alps for that matter, is not easily overlooked. An all-fabric, nonrigid airship might burn up *in toto* and leave few remains, but a Zeppelin has a substantial aluminum skeleton. The L-50 may have fallen into a body of water, possibly into the Mediterranean, but it seems that, at best, the partly deflated hydrogen cells would have kept it afloat for some time, and at worst, the surface would have been littered with floating debris.

When the Armistice was declared in November, 1918, the huge new Zeppelin L-72 was on the point of completion at the Zeppelin works in Fredrikshafen. Had the war continued many more months, the L-72 would have led two other advanced airships on a bombing raid on New York. In the spring of 1919, Captain Ernst Lehman (the most distinguished Zeppelin commander, later to die of burns after the *Hindenberg* disaster) readied the ship for a nonstop round trip trans-Atlantic flight. The German government, fearing that the Americans would consider the flight arrogant or threatening, ordered the plan abandoned. Later, the Versailles Treaty handed the L-72 over to France as part of war reparations.

In French hands, the ship, now named the *Dixmude*, turned in a number of notable endurance records. On December 18, 1923, the *Dixmude* took off for a flight over North Africa to establish yet more records. She was commanded by Commander du Plessis de Grenedah and carried a crew of forty, plus ten observers.

On December 21, the ship was sighted over Tunis, but a storm blew up and contact was lost for some time. On the 24th, the French government reported that it had received a radio message: the *Dixmude* was experiencing some engine trouble and the captain was looking for a landing place. On the same day, the ship was again reported over Tunis. She was believed to be out of fuel. On

December 27, the French government changed its story. The last radio signal from the *Dixmude* had been on the 21st, and the last reliable sighting had been on the 20th near Biskra, Algeria, some 250 miles southwest of Tunis. On the 26th, she was sighted again near Insalah in the Sahara. Insalah is near the geographical center of Algeria.

By this time, both the Mediterranean and the Sahara were being patrolled as thoroughly as possible. French authorities believed that the *Dixmude* was down in the desert, but on the 29th, a new piece of evidence was found—fishermen discovered the body of Commander du Plessis off Sicily. His watch was stopped at 2:30. After the discovery, a stationmaster on the island claimed to have seen a light over the sea at 2:30 A.M. on December 23. On the 31st, burned fragments of the control car were also found in the sea near Sicily.

This is puzzling to say the least. The assumption is that the *Dixmude* was destroyed by a hydrogen explosion or fire over the Mediterranean on December 23rd, but French patrols were already sweeping the sea on that date. One body and a few pieces of debris from a 700-foot Zeppelin with fifty aboard seems insufficient. There should have been at least several bodies, and a great quantity of wreckage. Furthermore, something was seen over Insalah on the 27th. If not the *Dixmude*, what was it?

No theory proposed seems to fit all the known facts. The best idea I can put forward is this: the *Dixmude*, like the British-American ZR-2 and the American *Shenandoah*, broke in two, with the bow burning, and the stern, with most of the crew aboard, drifting back over Africa and falling in the Sahara. Even this unlikely theory is not altogether satisfactory.

In May 1926, the Italian-built, Norwegian-owned, semirigid airship *Norge* (N-1) flew across the North Pole from Spitzbergen Island to Teller, Alaska. The ship was commanded by its designer, General Umberto Nobile, but the official heads of the expedition were Roald Amundsen and Lincoln Ellsworth. During and after the flight, personal friction between Amundsen and Nobile developed and eventually blew up to feud proportions. Nobile, feeling that he had been cheated of credit, prevailed on Mussolini to authorize an all-Italian polar airship expedition.

In May 1928, the new semirigid *Italia* (N-4) flew to Spitzbergen to begin an ambitious series of exploratory scientific flights over the Arctic. On May 23, the *Italia* set out for its first flight to the Pole. The *Italia* successfully overflew the Pole, dropping Italian flags, a crucifix blessed by the Pope, and making scientific observations. Nobile decided to return to Spitzbergen, but the ship found itself fighting headwinds and freezing fogs. On the morning of the 25th, overladen with ice, and with elevators jammed, the *Italia* crashed on the ice pack. The control gondola and the aft engine car were torn away, leaving ten men on the ice. The gas bag, with the keel corridor and two engines still attached, carried six other crewmen away.

After nearly a month on the ice, the survivors of the first crash succeeded in establishing radio contact with their supply ship. Eventually the eight survivors were brought safely back to Europe.

When the position of Nobile's party was first established, Roald Amundsen set out with a rescue party in a large seaplane. Over the Barents Sea, Amundsen's plane and party vanished; no trace was ever found. (When the *Norge* flew over the Pole, Nobile threw out a large Italian flag, which came near to fouling a propeller. Amundsen was heard to remark, "That man will be the death of me yet.") Nor was any trace ever found of the *Italia* or the six men aboard.

In the 1930s, the disasters that befell the R-101, the *Akron*, and the *Macon*, caused the abandonment of rigid airships by Britain and the U.S. Only the Germans' reliable old *Graf Zeppelin* and the new giant *Hindenberg* maintained the line. On May 6, 1937, fire destroyed the *Hindenberg* at Lakehurst, New Jersey. Public confidence in airships was utterly dashed. When World War II began, the old *Graf Zeppelin* and the *Hindenberg*'s new sister ship *Graf Zepplin II* were broken up by the Nazi government. Now only the helium-inflated nonrigid airships (blimps) of the United States Navy were left.

On August 16, 1942, the U.S. Navy blimp L-8 flew from

Moffett Field, California, on antisubmarine patrol. Aboard were Lieutenant Ernest Cody and Ensign Hank Adams, a survivor of the crash of the *Macon*. The little airship had left its mast at 6:00 A.M. At 7:50, Cody reported sighting an oil slick, and then no more radio signals were received from the L-8. Search planes were sent out, but a low cloud layer hampered the search. At 10:30, an airliner sighted the blimp in the San Francisco Bay area. Fifteen minutes later, the ship came down on a beach near Fort Funston. When fishermen tried to anchor the blimp, they saw that the cabin door was open, and no one was aboard. A gust of wind dragged the L-8 along the beach. It struck a cliff and a depth charge fell from its rack. Lightened, the airship rose again and drifted southeast. At 11:15, the L-8 came gently to earth just south of San Francisco, in a street of Daly City. She had been brought down by a leak apparently opened in the collision with the cliff. The two crewmen were not aboard, nor were the regulation life jackets, but all other equipment, including rescue and survival gear, was intact. Presumably the ship was abandoned within a few minutes after the oil slick report, but if the men had fallen at that point they would have been seen by surface ships nearby. If they had fallen later, the bodies, or at least the jackets, would have floated. Considering the poor visibility that day, it is conceivable that the flyers could have voluntarily landed the ship and debarked, but for them to do so without radioing would require some unknown and sinister motive. None can be reasonably suggested for either man. The navy could find no reasonable explanation for the loss of the crew of the L-8. It remains a mystery.

The Zeppelin is extinct, the blimp is a vanishing breed. It may be that the dirigible will disappear from the air in the next few years. But on the other hand, a small rigid airship of novel design is now being tested in New Jersey, and in Germany the Zeppelin idea is not altogether dead. The giant airship may fly again.

# OCEAN BOTTOM MYSTERIES
## Ronald J. Willis

*Ivan T. Sanderson recently published a book,* Invisible Residents *(Cleveland: World Publishing Company, 1970), in which he speculates that intelligent nonhuman beings may be living in the ocean.*

*The strange photograph described below may be a sign of activity of these beings.*

The photo on the cover [of *INFO Journal*, Vol. II, No. 3] was taken by a deep-sea camera at 13,500 feet by the oceanographic ship *Eltanin*, August 29, 1964, 1,000 miles west of Cape Horn. There has been speculation on what the thing is, including suggestions that it is some sort of machine or electronic device—artificial, but maybe not *man*-made.

Interesting as this theory is, we wonder if maybe the answer is that it's just a "new" type of animal. The *Umbellula*, a long-stemmed polyp about three feet high and bearing a cluster of hydra-like tentacles, bears a certain resemblance to the "thing" found by the *Eltanin*. A photograph of the *Umbellula* was taken by the oceanographic ship *Kane* at a depth of 15,900 feet some 350 miles west of the Cape of Good Hope. However, the *Umbellula* had been dredged up before the time this photograph was taken, probably when it was luminescent.

The ocean deeps turn out to be more populated than was previously thought. In the middle of the nineteenth century, it was assumed that the enormous pressure would prevent anything except the tiniest animacules from living below a few thousand feet. But as the *Challenger* expedition and succeeding ones scouted the deeps, more and more was turned up, until now it is clear that life exists down as far as we have investigated. The oceanographic ship *John Elliott Pillsbury* recently brought up out of the Puerto Rico Trench, from a depth of about five miles, a fish of the genus *Bassogigas*.

In the *Morning of the Magicians*, Pauwels and Bergier note a strange track found in the mud by oceanographic probes at 15,000 feet. We obtained copies of this photo, but additional photos have shown the creature making the track—a type of acorn worm.

So maybe our outlandish thing down there in the South Pacific is some sort of animal like the *Umbellula*. But then again—maybe not. There are some other strange stories of tracks way down there. In the Arctic Ocean, 400 miles from the pole, Dr. Kenneth Hunkins dropped a camera through the ice to a depth of 7,000 feet and got photos of "chicken tracks," 2½ inches long, ½ inch wide (*New York Times*, February 24, 1958). And in the Kermatek Trough, north of New Zealand, Nikita Zenkevitch got photos of "a big, unknown sea animal" at a depth of six miles (*Manchester Guardian*, March 19, 1958).

These two cases suggest that some rather strange things must be living down there. The thing photographed by the *Eltanin* may be an animal as strange as we know how to imagine.

# THE "TULLI PAPYRUS"

## Paul J. Willis

*This affair has never been cleared up. Contrary to what has been claimed, Prince Boris de Rachewiltz is not a myth; his daughter was the wife of the now deceased great American poet Ezra Pound.*

In the pages of *Doubt* (the Fortean Society magazine, No. 41, 1953, pages 214–15), Tiffany Thayer published what purported to be both a transcription and a translation of an Egyptian papyrus dating from the reign of Thothmes III (Eighteenth Dynasty, New Kingdom). The text as reproduced was a transcription from hieratic into hieroglyphics (with indicated lacunae). [The text, as reproduced in *Doubt*, can be found in the photo insert.]

This was said to have been sent to Thayer by Prince Boris de Rachewiltz, who wrote, "the transcription I send is from an original papyrus of the New Kingdom that I found among other papers and documents of the late Professor Alberto Tulli, former

55

Director of the Egyptian Vatican Museum. He brought those documents from Egypt, but his death left them untranslated and unpublished. It is due to the courtesy of his brother, Monsignor Gustavo, of the Vatican Archive that I had the opportunity to translate them.

"The present transcription is a part of the Royal Annals of the times of Thuthmosis III (1504–1450 circa b.c.) [sic] and the original is in very bad condition. The beginning and the end are missing, its writing (in hieratic) is pale and with several lacunae that I have reproduced in my Hyeroglyphic [sic] transcription with progressive numbers. . . . Of the whole papyrus (cm. 20 x 18) I have chosen the best preserved and perhaps the most interesting part. But it is up to you to judge it."

There follows de Rachewiltz's translation.

"In the year 22, third month of winter, sixth hour of the day (. . . 2 . . .) The scribas of the House of Life found it was a circle of fire that was coming in the sky. (Though) it had no head, the breath of its mouth (had) a foul odour. Its body 1 "rod" long and 1 "rod" large. It had no voice. Their hearts became confused through it: then they laid themselves on their bellies (. . . 3 . . .) They went to the King . . ? to report it. His Majesty ordered (. . . 4 . . .) has been examined (. . . 5 . . .) as to all which is written in the House of Life His Majesty was meditating upon what happened. Now, after some days had passed over those things, Lo! they were more numerous than anything. They were shining in the sky more than the sun to the limits of the four supports of heaven. (. . . 6 . . .) Powerful was the position of the fire circles. The army of the king looked on and His Majesty was in the midst of it. It was after supper. Thereupon they (i.e. the fire circles) went up higher directed to South. Fishes and volatiles fell down from the sky. (It was) a marvel never occurred since the foundation of this Land! Caused His Majesty to be brought incense to pacify the hearth (. . . 9 . . . To write?) what happened in the book of the House of Life (. . . 10 . . . to be remembered?) for the Eternity."

This text has since appeared in books (such as Harold T.

Wilkin's *Flying Saucers Uncensored*, London, 1956) as an example of an early record of a UFO observation and/or Fortean fall.

Now the crux of the story.

Does (or did) this papyrus exist? If it does (did) exist, where is it now?

De Rachewiltz identified the manuscript as having been in the collections of the Vatican.

Checking into the case, we read in Samuel Rosenberg's chapter "UFOs in History" in the *Condon Report*, that in answer to a cable to the Egyptian section of the Vatican Museum, this reply was received:

*"Papyrus Tulli not propriety [sic] [[Rosenberg's sic]] of Vatican Museum. Now it is dispersed and no more traceable."*

> *The Inspector to Egyptian Section*
> *Vatican Museum*
> *(signed) Gianfranco Nolli*
> *Vatican City, July 25, 1968*

Later Dr. Condon himself—or so we are told—wrote Dr. Walter Ramberg, scientific attaché at the U.S. Embassy in Rome.

Dr. Ramberg is quoted as responding: ". . . the current Director of the Egyptian Section of the Vatican Museum, Dr. Nolli, said that . . . Prof. Tulli had left all his belongings to a brother of his who was a priest in the Lateran Palace. Presumably the famous papyrus went to this priest. Unfortunately the priest died also in the meantime and his belongings were dispersed among heirs, who may have disposed of the papyrus as something of little value.

"Dr. Nolli intimated that Prof. Tulli was only an amateur 'Egyptologist' [the quotation marks are in text; evidently Dr. Ramberg is not sure that Egyptologists are really scientists] and that Prince de Rachewiltz is no expert either. He suspects that Tulli was taken in and that the papyrus is a fake. . . ."

We made inquiries of our own, not related to the Condon material, to both the Vatican and to St. Louis University, where the Pius XII Memorial Library houses microfilm copies of the Vatican

Library. From the latter (personal letter, February 10, 1970, from Charles J. Ermatinger, Vatican Microfilm Librarian, Pius XII Memorial Library), we learned that St. Louis University does not have microfilms of the Vatican's Egyptian papyri.

But from the Vatican itself, we received answer from Mons. Nolli himself. The gist of the letter to us is that Monsignor Nolli spoke personally with de Rachewiltz, and he makes these points: (1) the Tulli Papyrus never has been in the collections of the Vatican; (2) the papyrus was seen by Professor Tulli in 1934 in the hands of the Cairo antiquarian Tano; (3) the transcription from hieratic into hieroglyphics was done by E. Drioton; (4) Drioton's opinion was that the papyrus was not of a "magic" character, but described the fall of a meteorite [interesting meteorite]; (5) Tulli did not acquire the papyrus because of an excessive asking price, but conceivably it could have been acquired by the Cairo Museum later, or it could still be in the hands of Tano.

Note that the general implication of this letter is not that the papyrus is (or was) a fake as hinted in the statement of Dr. Ramberg.

But where does this leave us?

Nowhere in particular. The "Papiro meteorologico" or "Papiro Tulli" may have been authentic. It may still exist. If it does, and it actually reads as de Rachewiltz averred, it is still highly unclear as to the nature of the events referred to.

One lesson is to be gathered from the papyrological morass, however: the skepticism which Rosenberg advocates is very well merited—and one may just as well advocate an equal skepticism both in regard to the Vatican and to the advisors of the *Condon Report*. We may all profit by following Rosenberg "in regarding no opinion as certain."

*Despite doubts expressed about him in the* Condon Report, *de Rachewiltz seems to have a certain scientific reputation. He even has a genuine address: The Ludwig Keimer Foundation for Comparative Research in Archeology and Ethnology, Elisabethenstrasse 15, 4000 Basel, Switzerland.*

*Rachewiltz, without denying the existence of the Tulli Papyrus, challenges the accuracy of the translation attributed to him and especially the interpretation given of it. According to him, nothing warrants the statement that a raid by extraterrestrial beings is involved here.*

*Other researchers have compared the (translated) text of the Tulli Papyrus with the biblical text that describes "wheels of fire" appearing at the time the prophet Ezekiel was mysteriously carried away.*

*The question is still open.*

# THE ROBOZER MIRACLE
## Jacques Bergier

*The Soviet Union has been the setting for a great number of strange events. From my extensive documentation on the subject I have selected an enigma that is three centuries old: the miracle of Robozer. My selection is based on three reasons:*

*1. To the best of my knowledge, nothing has been written in the West on the subject; thus my contribution to this book is a completely unpublished document;*

*2. The bona fide Commission of Contacts, a semiofficial organization established by the Soviet magazine* Knowledge and Power, *feels that this phenomenon should be studied;*

*3. My principal reason is that, despite all the efforts of the nineteenth-century rationalist thinkers and of more broad-minded Soviet scientists, the mystery of Robozer has remained unsolved for three centuries. Science will surely find an explanation for it some day, but in the meantime it poses a major problem.*

It happened at Robozer, the site of a monastery in the Moscow area, in the year 7171 after the creation of the world, according to the Orthodox Church of Most Holy Russia, in 1663 of what we call the Christian era and the Soviets, who do not believe in Jesus Christ, call simply "the modern age."

The exact date was August 15, a Saturday (according to the Gregorian calendar). The ecclesiastical authorities immediately questioned the witnesses, two of whom—Ivachko Rjevski, an agricultural laborer, and Levka Fiedorov, a peasant who worked his own land—were less terrified than the others, and gave similar descriptions.

According to these descriptions, immense flames appeared over an area approximately 450 feet wide, at the height of the day and under a clear and cloudless sky, on Lake Robozer, a small lake about one and one-quarter miles wide. The flames were crowned with blue smoke, and two glowing lights shot up from the phenomenon.

The flames disappeared for the space of an hour, then reappeared approximately 1,650 feet from their original location. Ten minutes later, they disappeared again, and then reappeared once more. They were accompanied by a terrible noise and gave off an intense heat that prevented spectators from approaching in boats. Many fish were killed, others were seen escaping. After the phenomenon, the lake was covered with a reddish coating similar to rust.

A second examination by the ecclesiastical authorities was held on November 30 of the same year, with the same results. The full text of these examinations was published in 1842 by an archaeological commission that examined the archives of the Monastery of Saint Cyril of Robozer.

According to the evidence given in the second examination, the height of the phenomenon was 131 feet, in modern terms. One of the witnesses stated that the light given off was so intense that the bottom of the lake (which is about 26 feet deep at that point) could be seen. Several witnesses had been standing under the porch of the monastery. Others who had tried to approach the flames in a boat had received slight burns.

Needless to say, numerous hypotheses have been proposed, but none of them has withstood examination. The first of these was that it was a mirage, a phenomenon that was already well known at that time. But a mirage does not transmit enough energy to cause burns, and it does not leave behind a thick coat of a metal oxide that resembles rust.

At the beginning of the nineteenth century, when the work of Chladni had proved the existence of meteorites despite Lavoisier's rationalist skepticism, an attempt was made to find the explanation of the Robozer enigma in a meteorite. But no debris had been found. Moreover, once a meteorite has fallen it does not later reappear twice. A meteorite falls at the rate of about 32 feet per second per second. The Robozer ball of fire continued for a time; for an hour and a half during its first appearance, the water itself burned, that is, it decomposed into hydrogen and oxygen, which united explosively.

The meteorite theory was energetically defended by D. O. Swiatsky in 1915, in a pamphlet published in Petrograd (now Leningrad), but it has been completely demolished by all the experts.

Another theory concerns collision with a comet, but it stands up no better than the preceding theory—the comet would have been minuscule. Moreover, if a comet collided with the earth, this would, again, be an instantaneous phenomenon and would not last for an hour and a half.

Modern rationalists immediately dredged up the hypothesis of ball lightning. It was shown to be impossible, but it is very popular right now. Professor Kapitza has reproduced it in his laboratory and has made very beautiful photographs of it. Ball lightning is a plasmodium, that is, it is ionized, electrically charged matter held together by forces that are as yet unknown. But ball lightning has a maximum existence of five seconds, and does not exceed ten inches. If the Robozer phenomenon had been ball lightning, it would have been most exceptional lightning and, scientifically speaking, completely impossible.*

---

*This definition, however, represents only one view of ball lightning. It ignores probably ninety percent of the phenomena associated with ball lightning. —Paul J. Willis

Moreover, ball lightning is linked with storms, and is probably produced by ordinary lightning. The Robozer miracle occurred under a cloudless sky devoid of any storm. Moreover, observations have been made of ball lightning falling into water. One of these observations, in which the rise in temperature of a container of water into which the ball had fallen was measured with a thermometer, has since then served as a basis for estimating the energy in ball lightning.

In none of these observations was a layer of rust ever seen to appear on the surface of the water. This would be impossible, moreover, since ball lightning is composed of ionized nitrogen and oxygen and electrons. Thus it contains no iron, and hence it cannot leave any iron deposits.

Yuri Rostzius of the Contacts Commission has seriously but prudently proposed the hypothesis of an automatic interplanetary probe from another inhabited world that may have crashed on the earth as the result of a technical accident. The Robozer miracle may thus have come from outer space.

The hypothesis is not unpleasant.

However, even if it did come from outside, it is possible that the Robozer miracle was not conscious. A small fragment of antimatter may have struck the surface of the lake and exploded upon contact with the water. A cosmic particle of exceptional energy may have fallen at that spot.

The studies must now be continued. "After three centuries?" the skeptics will ask. After three centuries the lake is still there. It can be determined whether or not its bottom contains ore that could rise to the surface and leave a layer of rust. If it does not, there will be a strong presumption that the type of rust found on the surface of the lake was produced by the combustion of the surface of a machine. It is possible, furthermore, that this machine was able to start again after two unsuccessful attempts and after it had lost a portion of its surface by ablation. Terrestrial space capsules returning from space lose a large part of their surface in this way, but the spacemen nevertheless survive.

Other interplanetary explanations that do not involve a machine are also conceivable. The Robozer object may have been a superintense cosmic particle that produced transmutation by sheaves of subparticles it emitted when it struck the earth. It could also have been a fragment of antimatter that produced an intense liberation of energy and, from this liberation, a plasmodium that reformed twice before being dissipated.

In the spirit of Charles Fort, we can also envision a door opening onto another universe. We shall not talk of parallel universes, precisely for the reason that parallel lines do not meet. But legends abound concerning another universe that can open onto ours.

I feel that we have now covered all conceivable hypotheses concerning the Robozer miracle. The true solution perhaps lies beyond the radius of action of our imagination.

I know of no other example reproducing the same phenomena —not on earth, at any rate. Fairly long luminous eruptions have been observed on Mars. Other luminous eruptions have been observed on the moon. The Soviet astronomer Nikolai Kozirev succeeded in examining the light emitted and found carbon compounds corresponding to a flame with a very high temperature. These emissions have been noted in a large number of lunar craters. Perhaps we are dealing here with a phenomenon that is the same as the Robozer miracle.

Mars has a very diluted atmosphere composed chiefly of nitrogen and carbonic gas, which could, if brought up to sufficiently high temperature, form a luminous ball. There is no atmosphere on the moon, and it is thought that the incandescent gases observed by Kozirev came from inside the moon. What force could have brought them to a state of incandescence? As in the Robozer case, we do not know. A stream of energy coming from a laser would obviously be one explanation, but *who* is operating this interplanetary laser? It is very difficult to say.

The reader is requested, under pain of corporal punishment, not to tell me that it was a flying saucer that exploded at Robozer! Since there are no flying saucers, how could one of these nonexistent machines have exploded?

It is equally foolish to tell me that the Czar's subjects were carrying on nuclear experiments. This seems extremely improbable.

Furthermore, there is no mention of any alchemist or magician in the history of the region. The inhabitants seem to have been good Christians and faithful subjects of their father, the Czar.

Obviously it would be interesting to learn whether a major magnetic storm occurred on August 15, 1663. It is not impossible that we shall one day find out, because methods of detecting magnetic storms that occurred in the past are now beginning to be devised.

These disturbances leave traces in ores. Their study is called paleomagnetism, a recognized science that owes a great deal to the French Nobel prize winner Louis Néel. If there was a shift of the magnetic poles on August 15, 1663, we shall learn about it, and it will tend to prove that an immense energy was released. Science has not said its last word, and probably some day soon we shall learn a part of the truth about Robozer.

Perhaps we shall learn the full truth if, one day, through contact with extraterrestrial beings, we learn that an exploratory astroship broke down on earth on August 15, 1663, of our calendar.

# PART THREE
## STRANGE CREATURES

# "THE DEVIL'S HOOFMARKS"
# AN UNSOLVED ENIGMA

## Paul J. Willis

Much has been written on this subject—too much, some will say—so I will not weary the reader with more than an initial reminder as to the occurrence in question. On the morning of February 8, 1855, the inhabitants of a wide area in south Devonshire awoke to find the snow on the ground was crossed by an enormous number of strange tracks, small, hoof-like in appearance, and of incredible multiplicity. There were, quite possibly, more than 100 miles of tracks (5; p. 18)!

The general appearance of the tracks can be gathered from the drawings below, based on the drawing depicted in the *Illustrated London News* (March 3, 1855; p. 214), and showing this drawing viewed from both directions. The individual prints measured about 4 inches long by 2¾ inches wide and had a constant separation of 8 to 8½ inches. The tracks were in a straight line.

What made them? Explanations have been advanced ranging from kangaroos to birds. (There is a rather subliminal idea in certain heads that a tourist from a visiting extraterrestial spacecraft

69

left them—I seem to recall that the late Harold T. Wilkins toyed with this idea. For obvious reasons, this theory has yet to find any supporters among the ranks of professional zoologists.)

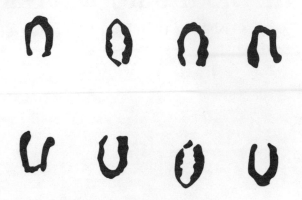

Figure 4. The "devil's hoofmarks" from the *Illustrated London News.*

There are a few points in relation to the problem of identifying *what* made the tracks that have, in my opinion, not been sufficiently well emphasized in past accounts, i.e., not often enough, nor in a complete conjunction. I now present them for consideration.

(*A*) If the tracks are to be attributed to any known terrestrial animal (including birds), the most difficult (therefore important) part to explain is the fantastic *placement*, i.e.: "This mysterious visitor generally only passed *once* down or across each garden or courtyard, and did so in nearly all the houses in many parts of the several towns above mentioned, as also in the farms scattered about; this regular track passing in some instances over the roofs of houses, and hayricks, and very high walls (one 14 feet), without displacing the snow on either side or altering the distance between the feet, and passing on as if the wall had not been any impediment. The gardens with high fences or walls, and gates locked, were equally visited as those open and unprotected. . . . A scientific acquaintance informed me of his having traced the same prints across a field up to a haystack. The surface of the stack was wholly free from marks of any kind, but on the opposite side of the stack, in a direction exactly corresponding with the tracks thus traced, the prints began again! The same fact has been ascertained in respect of a wall intervening . . . Two other gentlemen, resident in the same parish, pursued a line of prints during three hours and a half, marking their progress under gooseberry bushes and espalier fruit trees; and then missing them, regained sight of the impression on the roofs of some houses to which their march of investigation brought them. . . ." (7) The tracks are also recorded as having passed through "a circular opening of one foot diameter" and "through a six-inch pipe drain." (7) The tracks appeared to cross an estuary of the sea two miles wide.

It will do no good to say that more than one animal was responsible (such a conclusion seems inevitable anyway)—it will not explain how any known animal, in whatever quantity, could seem to "pass through walls" or cross rooftops as though such were no obstacle at all, and seemingly also to have the ability to pass through small holes less than a foot wide. Also of note, as I gather from the accounts, the tracks seem not to reverse themselves or wander very circuitously—something rather bizarre in itself, I should say.

(*B*) "The effect of the atmosphere upon these marks is given by many as a solution; but how could it be possible for the atmosphere to affect one impression and not another? On the morning that the above were observed, the snow bore the fresh marks of cats, dogs, rabbits, birds, and men clearly defined. Why, then, should a continuous track, far more clearly defined—so clearly even, that the raising in the centre of the frog of each foot could be plainly seen—why then should this particular mark be the only one which was affected by the atmosphere, and all the others left as they were?

"Besides, the most singular circumstance connected with it was that this particular mark removed the snow, wherever it appeared, clear, as if cut with a diamond, or branded with a hot iron; of course, I am not alluding to its appearance after having been trampled on, or meddled with by the curious in and about the thoroughfares of the towns. In one instance this track entered a covered shed, and passed through it out of a broken part of the wall at the other end, where the atmosphere could not affect it.

"The writer of the above has passed a five months' winter in the backwoods of Canada, and has had much experience in tracking wild animals and birds upon the snow, and can safely say he has never seen a more clearly-defined track, or one that appeared to be less affected by the atmosphere. . . ." (7)

The above circumstance is quite baffling. Ordinary prints in snow, of course, are made by pressure, and exhibit clear signs of compression in the snow around the print. Were these in truth made by the *removal* of snow? How can one account for that fact?

(*C*) One associated detail—noted by Fort, but nowhere else that I have found—is that, according to one description (though made about 35 years after the event), the Devonshire tracks alternated at "huge but regular intervals with what seemed to be the impressions of the point of a stick." (4;16) What bearing this may have is wildly problematical.

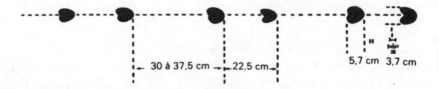

30 à 37,5 cm — 22,5 cm    5,7 cm  3,7 cm

Figure 5. Russell's 1945 tracks from Belgium.

(*D*) Fort (4), Gould (5), Heuvelmans (6), and Russell (20) have pointed out curiously similar reports from widely separated geographical localities. I will not go into details, especially since several, or all, of these reports may well have no particular relevance to the Devonshire case. I list the incidents recorded: Scotland, 1839-40 (13; quoted in 4); Kerguelen Island, Indian

Ocean, 1840 (*Voyage of Discovery and Research in the Southern and Antarctic Regions*, Vol. 1, p. 87, Capt. Sir James Clark Ross; cited in 5); Poland, ca. 1855 (10); Belgium, 1945 (3;20); Brazil, before 1954 (6); also in Fort (4) are references to incidents that may or may not be pertinent. One (p. 246, ref. to *Philosophical Transactions*, pp. 50–500) is a report that "after the quake of July 15, 1757, upon the sands of Penzance, Cornwall, in an area of more than 100 square yards, were found marks like hoof prints, except that they were not crescentic." (Note the proximity to Devonshire. The Brazilian tracks were not crescentic either.) An even more obscure reference is made (p. 215; from *Notes and Queries*, 9-6-225) to a report from the Chinese annals that reads like the Devonshire accounts: "of a courtyard of a palace—dwellers of the palace waking up one morning, finding the courtyard marked with tracks like the footprints of an ox—supposed that the devil did it." Attention is called to the fact that some of these accounts in no way involve *snow*, but tracks found in sand or mud.

On July 10, 1953, the *New York Herald Tribune*, "Just About Everything," by William Chapman White, carried the account of a tale from Burnham-on-Crouch, in Essex. It seems that the headmaster of a local boys' camp had promised his charges that a magician who would be visiting them would have as part of his act "five wild unmanageable kangaroos." The magician had no kangaroos, but the headmaster seized on this sensationalism in order to arouse the boys' expectations for an otherwise very un-novel type of performance. When the magician arrived, he connived with an explanation—his kangaroos had escaped. As soon as this news came to the notice of people in the surrounding countryside, the headmaster began receiving reports from persons who had "seen" the kangaroos from as far as 20 miles away!

Some of the theories used to explain the "Devil's hoofmarks" in a certain way remind one of the headmaster's explanation of the missing kangaroos—suggest an animal, and there will be facts to fit the explanation. But unfortunately not enough of the facts.

One might also recall Fort's beautiful sardonicism (4; p. 307): "My own acceptance is that not less than a thousand one-legged kangaroos, each shod with a very small horseshoe, could have marked that snow of Devonshire."

## References

*This bibliography does not pretend to be exhaustive in the sense that everything published on the subject is mentioned. Purely derivative material has been ignored, but to the best of my knowledge everything written that is of any consequential originality has been included.*

(1) Burton, Maurice. *Animal Legends*, "Problem Prints in Snow." Frederick Muller, London, 1955.

(2) ———. "More Mysterious" ("Nature Notes"). *The Daily Telegraph & Morning Post*, London, January 2, 1965.

(3) *Doubt, The Fortean Society Magazine.* No. 15, New York, n.d. Article on Eric Frank Russell's report from Belgium, 1945. (See also 20.) *Reproduces measurements of tracks, which are smaller and differently spaced in comparison with the Devonshire tracks.*

(4) Fort, Charles. *The Book of the Damned.* Chapter 28, pp. 305–10. (New York: Henry Holt, 1941). *Together with Gould (5), probably the best accounts.*

(5) Gould, Rupert T. *Oddities, A Book of Unexplained Facts.* Chaper 1, pp. 9–22. 3rd edition. University Books, New Hyde Park, New York, 1965.

(6) Heuvelmans, Bernard. *On the Track of Unknown Animals.* Pp. 323–25. Hill and Wang, New York, 1959. *Relates accounts of the tracks of the* pe de garrafa. *Dr. Heuvelmans informed me (in a letter dated May 24, 1966) that he had received "no further data" since the publication of this book.*

(7) *Illustrated London News.* February 24, 1855, p.187.

(8) ———. March 3, 1855, p. 214.

(9) ———. March 10, 1855, p. 238.

(10) ———. March 17, 1855, p. 242.

(11) Leutscher, Alfred G. "The devil's Hoof-marks—A Solution to a Hundred-year-old Mystery." *Journal of Zoology*, London, 148, pp. 381–83, 1966. *Mr. Leutscher has come out for the wood*

*mouse as the perpetrator of the Devonshire tracks. Dr. Burton (letter to the author, June 21, 1966) says that although he considers "Mr. Leutscher's hypothesis is the most promising to date" that "since he put forward his theory I have taken note of the tracks of this mouse in snow and looking at these it seems most unlikely that anybody could have become excited by them or have interpreted them in the way they were interpreted."*

(12) ———. "The Devil's Hoof-marks." *Animals*, Vol. 6, No. 8, April 20, 1965, pp. 208-9. *One need only point out that it is hard to conceive how mice could jump onto rooftops, or over 14-foot walls.*

(13) *London Times*. March 14, 1840. (Quoted in Fort, p. 310.)

(14) ———. February 16, 1855. (Quoted in Gould, pp. 9–11.)

(15) ———. March 6, 1855, p. 9.

(16) *Notes and Queries*. 7-8-508.

(17) ———. 7-9-18.

(18) ———. 7-9-70.

(19) ———. 7-9-253.

(20) Russell, Eric Frank. *Great World Mysteries*. Chapter 3, "Satan's Footprints." Pp. 28-45. Roy Publishers, New York, 1957.

# THE DEVIL WALKS AGAIN

## Vincent Gaddis

To add to the data in the article "The Devil's Hoofmarks," by Paul J. Willis in *INFO* (Vol. I, No. 1), I submit the following case published in *Tomorrow*, Autumn, 1957. The article is entitled "Did the Devil Walk Again?"

It was written by Dr. Eric J. Dingwall, the English scholar and author, a close collaborator of the late Dr. Alfred Kinsey, and well known for his work in anthropology and psychical research. "Of all the strange stories to which I have listened," writes Dr. Dingwall, "[this one] was one of the oddest and the most inexplicable."

The story was told by a man identified only as "Mr. Wilson." A native of England, Wilson had come to America as a young man and operated a successful business in New York. After the stock market crash, however, he lost a large amount of money. He returned to England where he settled in a village and in due time became the proprietor of a small but profitable business concern.

One day, in a British magazine, he read an article about the Devil's Hoofmarks of Devon in 1855. He had never heard of the mystery before. Since Dr. Dingwall's name was mentioned in the article, Wilson sent him a letter. Previously, Wilson had been so disturbed by his experience that he had only confided it to three trusted friends.

Dr. Dingwall went to Wilson's office to interview him. He found Wilson to be a tall, solidly built man with a practical mind. He was "obviously no imaginative dreamer of tall stories."

It was in October, 1950, Wilson said, when he decided to take a vacation trip to the Devonshire west coast town where he had spent his youth. On the final day of his stay, he went to look at his old home and visit the beach where he had played as a child. This small beach is entirely enclosed by steep cliffs. The entrance is a narrow passage between and under two huge rocks, its opening barred by a tall iron gate. In summer persons using the beach are charged a fee at the gate. But on this gloomy autumn afternoon, the gate had been locked for the winter.

Mr. Wilson's boyhood home was nearby. He remembered that it was possible to reach the beach by going through the garden of the house and through another passage. Taking this route, he was soon standing on the sands of the deserted beach. The sea had been to the top of the beach, but when he arrived, the tide had gone out, leaving the sand as smooth as glass. It was then that Wilson made his bewildering discovery.

Starting at the top of the beach, just below a perpendicular cliff, and going in a straight line down the center of the beach and into the sea, were a series of prints in the sand. They were sharply defined—"almost as if cut out by some sharp instrument." About six feet apart, they appeared to be the hoofmarks of some biped and resembled those that might have been made by a large unshod pony. They were not cloven. The impressions were deeper than the footprints made by Wilson, who weighs some 200 pounds.

One circumstance that especially puzzled Wilson was that no sand splashed up along the edges of the prints—"it looked as if each mark had been cut out of the sand with a flat iron." He tried to match them with his own stride by walking beside them, then tried to jump the distance from one mark to another, but they were too far apart even though he is a tall man with long legs. There was no returning track from the sea, and there were rocky headlands on each side of the narrow beach.

Dr. Dingwall asks some unanswered questions: What possible creature, from land or water, could have made these prints? What size could it have been to have so long a stride? What kind of hoof could make so clear-cut an impression? If it was a sea animal, why should it have hard hooves? If it were a land animal, why did it enter the sea? Or did it have wings?

Mr. Wilson said the tracks were fresh, for the receding tide was only just beyond the last print in the line. What would he have seen if he had arrived just a little earlier?

Dr. Dingwall writes that similar strange footprints were seen in 1908 in the United States along the New Jersey coast from Newark to Cape May. They were attributed to the "Jersey Devil." He states: "Here again were reports of marks like the hooves of a pony in the thick snow, and again we have the story of how the tracks led up to wire fences and then continued on the other side, even when the uprights were only a few inches apart."

In conclusion, Dr. Dingwall says that the more questions one asks the more baffling does this mystery become.

# ENCOUNTERS WITH
# THE MATAH KAGMI*

## Tawani Wakawa

*The American abominable woodsmen, like the Tibetan abominable snowmen and the Malayan abominable men, create an annoying problem. Tibet and Malaysia still have areas that have been only slightly explored, and in any event one should beware of the traveler's tales. However, the various reports discussed below are too numerous and too precise to warrant a belief that the American abominable woodsman is only a legend.*

My Grandfather was born in upper California Country near the mountain of Shasta. This was in the year of 1853. He fought in the Modoc Indian War (1872–73) in defense of his homeland; however, it was the same old story—defeat, and being sent to a reservation.

Grandfather did not like the white man's reservation, however, and soon returned to the part of the country that he loved. It was

*Taken from *Many Smokes*, the National American Indian Magazine, Fall 1968.

by some very good luck and the help of a white friend in Yreka, California, he was able to buy some land near Tulelake up in the mountains. He then built a cabin there, and lived there from then on until his death. He died in 1935. He fell asleep on a river bank and never awakened again.

Grandfather lived a long and eventful life, but not always a happy one.

He told me this story as a child, and I never tired of hearing it. His first contact with the Sasquatch was one evening in the summer of 1897. He was walking along a deer trail near a lake just about dusk, when he saw up ahead something that looked like a tall bush. Upon coming a little closer, he became aware of a strong odor, sort of musky. He then gave a close look at the bush, and suddenly realized that it was not a bush at all, for it was covered from head to foot with thick coarse hair, much like horsehair. He took a step closer, but the creature made a sound that sounded like "Ny-yaaaah!" Grandfather now knew that this was one of the ones that he had heard the old ones tell about—a Sasquatch!

Although it was growing darker, Grandfather was able to see quite clearly two soft brown eyes through the hairy head part, then the creature moved slightly, and Grandfather made a motion of friendship and laid down the string of fish that he had been carrying. The creature evidently understood this, as it quickly snatched up the fish and struck out through the timber nearby. It stopped only for a moment and made a sound that Grandfather never forgot—a long, low "Aaagoooooooouummmm!"

Grandfather never told anyone outside the family this story, and he called them people. He referred to them as people called MATAH KAGMI. Now here is something that is most interesting, and doubtful that it could be by chance, and that is that the people in Tibet call the so-called snowman Metoh Kangmi. The two names are very much alike.

It was only a few weeks after his encounter with the Matah Kagmi that he was awakened one morning by some strange noises outside his cabin. Upon investigating, he found a stack of deer-skins fresh and ready for tanning. Off in the distance he heard that strange sound once again, "Aaagooooooouummmm!" After this there were other items left from time to time, such as wood for fuel, and wild berries and fruits.

It was a few years later that Grandfather had his second, but far more amazing contact with the Sasquatch. Grandfather had taken a job with some white men from the San Francisco area to help them search for some treasure that was supposed to be on Mount Shasta.

Now Grandfather never cared much for money, but times had changed for the Indian and living off the land was a little harder now. However these men had a map of some kind and were bound that they would find the gold in question, so Grandfather agreed to act as guide for them. However he could scarcely conceal the fact that he thought all whites a little crazy that searched for this yellow metal. Even though they assured Grandfather that if they found the gold he would be a rich man, this made little or no difference to him.

After the treasure party had reached the foot of Mount Shasta, the whites began drinking a lot, so Grandfather told them that he would go ahead and explore some of the lower level rock shelves, as they were in no condition to do so themselves. So on that morning he set out up a mountain trail, and after quite a bit of rough climbing, he reached a shelf that he wished to examine. Then it happened. He was struck in the leg by a timber rattler!

Grandfather killed the snake and started to come back down to a more comfortable spot, but soon found it difficult to go on, and as best as he can remember, he became sick at his stomach and fainted. When he came around again, he thought he was dreaming, for he was surrounded by three large Sasquatch about eight to ten feet tall. He noted that they had made a small cut on the snakebite and had somehow removed some of the venom, and placed cool moss on the bite. Then one of the Matah Kagmi made a kind of grunting sound, and the other two lifted him up and took him down a trail that he did not know. Finally after some little descent down the mountain side, they placed him under a low brushy tree and left. Again Grandfather heard that mournful cry of the Sasquatch, "Aaagooooooouummmm!"

After a while he began to feel better, and then took his old 44 caliber cap and ball pistol and began to fire some shots in the air. Finally the gold party found him. Grandfather said nothing about what happened concerning the Sasquatch. He was then taken back to where the pack mules were tied, and then on to the nearest little townlet where he rested a few days, and then returned to Tulelake. Grandfather told only his immediate family about this encounter, and after this would-never take anyone for any amount of money to the Mount Shasta region. He would only say: "Matah Kagmi live! That Holy Place, I have friends there."

For many years after, in the still of the evening or sometimes late at night, he would still hear the sound he now knew, "Aaagoooooooouummmm," the call of the Sasquatch. Grandfather went on to relate that the Matah Kagmi were not vicious, but were very shy, especially of the white man, and they generally only came out in the evenings and at night. They lived chiefly on roots they dug and berries, and only ate meat in the bitterest of cold weather. Their homes are in the deep burroughs of mountainsides, unknown to man.

I never tired of these stories that my Grandfather told to me as a boy, and he said they were true, and I believe him. May his spirit always know peace.

Acambaro figurines.
Courtesy INFO.

Acambaro figurines. Courtesy INFO.

*INFO*

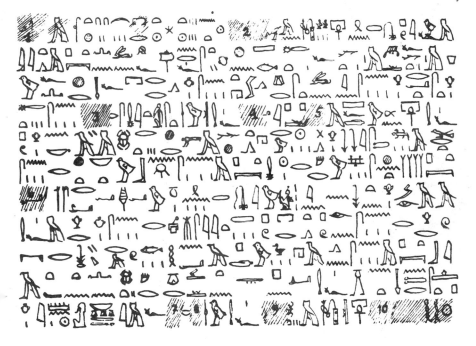

The "Tulli Papyrus." Reproduced from *Doubt*,
no. 41 (1953).

The Coso artifact (exterior view of the two halves).

g. B

The Coso artifact (interior view of the two halves).

Fig. C

Fig. D

The metal structure inside the Coso artifact, seen in profile. X-ray photograph courtesy Ronald C. Calais.

y photograph of the Coso artifact (frontal view),
ving a metal structure.

The dirigible "Dixmude." Photo Harlingue.

Bas-relief of the entrance gate of Babylon.
Photo courtesy Roger Viollet.

# SOME BIGFOOT TRADITIONS
# OF THE NORTH AMERICAN TRIBES

## Loren E. Coleman & Mark A. Hall

A vast folklore and a belief in a race of very primitive people with revolting habits is found from northern California up into the Arctic lands themselves. This tradition covers not only the whole stretch of the Pacific coast but also much of the rugged territory to the east, even into Greenland. Generally, these subhominids are described as very tall, fully haired, and retiring. Sometimes they are described as carnivorous.

To study this tradition, however, a note at the beginning must be made of the folklore of northeastern Asia. Among the Chuckchee, Bogoras (1902) finds *kele₁*—evil spirits—and *kele₂*—tribes of ancient times or cannibals. No sharp dividing line is to be found between these two words. However, Bogoras discovers that in the North American Eskimo terms with the same meanings—respectively, *tornait* (singular, *tornaq*) and *tornit* (singular, *tuneq*)—there exists a sharp division in import.

In Alaska (specifically Point Barrow), Spencer (1959, p.259) observes:

The western Eskimo appear not to have developed the rather elaborate views, found in the central and eastern regions, of a race of elder beings, those often referred to as the *tornait*. The term, however, is cognate with *tunarat*, which in North Alaska refers specifically to the powers of the shaman.

Spencer seems to have confused *tornit*, the ancient tribe, with *tornait*, the spirits that rule objects (sometimes called upon by the shamans). He (1959, p.261) does record that "giants were also part of the local terrain. They had no special powers, were simply 'big men' . . . They were regarded as timid and avoided contact with other men." These do have traits in common with the *tornit* of the East, and one wonders as to the source of Spencer's confusion. Boas (1964, pp.226-227) relates the tales from the central Eskimo on the *tornit:*

> In olden times the Inuit (i.e. the Eskimo) were not the only inhabitants of the country in which they live at the present time. Another tribe similar to them shared their hunting ground . . . The Tornit were much taller than the Inuit and had very long legs and arms. Almost all of them were blear eyes. They were extremely strong and could lift large boulders, which were by far too heavy for the Inuit.
> . . . . . . . . . . . . . . . . . . . . . . . . . . . . . . . . . . . . . . . . . . . . . . .
> They made neither kayaks nor bows.
> . . . . . . . . . . . . . . . . . . . . . . . . . . . . . . . . . . . . . . . . . . . . . . .
> The Tornit could not clean the sealskins so well as the Inuit, but worked them up with part of the blubber attached. Their way of preparing meat was disgusting, since they let it become putrid and placed it between the thigh and the belly to warm it.
> The old stone houses of the Tornit can be seen everywhere. Generally they did not build snow houses, but lived the whole winter in stone buildings, the roofs of which were frequently supported by whale ribs.

The *Tornit* are to be designated from traditions relating to the Indians who are called *Adla* or *Equigdleq*, i.e., Half-dogs, (Boas

1879). Kroeber (1899) tells of the *Tornit* tales from the Smith Sound Eskimos and notes that they are a frequent element in Greenland texts. He also learned of the *Tutuatin*, a fabulous being with tangled hair; although the true importance of this creature is unknown, it may be part of the *Tornit* tradition under a different name.

Observing that the Akudnirmiut (the inhabitants of Akudnirn) call the *Tornit* the "*Tuniqdjuait*," Boas (1964) goes on to note the Eskimo there as well as in Labrador considered the *Tornit* somewhat similar to themselves. "In Greenland they are entirely a fabulous tribe, each individual being of enormous size, living inland, and seldom hunting in the upper parts of the fjords" (Boas 1964, p.232). From northern Baffin Land, the *Tornit* are referred to as the *Toonijuk* and appear to be similar in many traits (very large, possess disgusting habits). Some clue to the fate of these beings is reflected by their temperament:

> Toonijuk were not dangerous; on the contrary they were timid and terribly afraid of dogs; they were also stupid and slow-going. The Pond Inlet Eskimos say that these big people never attacked Eskimos but fought among themselves until they killed each other off (but other Eskimo tribes claim to have stalked the stupid giants and killed them one by one, like game). They disappeared from the Canadian Arctic long before the memory of the oldest Eskimo, and only dim, distorted shreds of tales remain. When Idlouk was asked when the Toonijuk were here he could only answer, "Long ago, before my grandfather was born." That means, to an Eskimo, beyond memory.
>
> From grandmother to grandchild have come out of the dark past a few derelict tales of despised, repugnant sub-humans (Scherman 1956, pp.158-159).

The *Tornit* of the Eskimo is a widespread tradition of giant prehumans that existed in former times which is complemented by similar tales.

The Mahoni, who flit through the Peel River Country in

the northern Yukon, are enormous hairy giants with red eyes, who eat human flesh and devour entire birch trees at a gulp. The predatory Sasquatches of British Columbia's mountain caves are eight feet tall and covered with black woolly hair from head to foot. There are others, all kin to these: the terrible Brush Man of the Loucheaux in the upper Mackenzie, with his black face and yellow eyes, preying on women and children; the Weetigo of the Barrens, that horrible naked cannibal, his face black with frostbite, his lips eaten away to expose his fanglike teeth; the eight-foot head-hunting "Mountain Men" of the Nahanni; and those imaginary beings of Great Slave Lake whom the Dogrib Indians simply call "the Enemy" and fear so greatly that they must always build their homes on islands safe from the shoreline where the Enemy roam (Berton 1956, pp. 10–11).

From the east to the west coast of Canada and the northern United States, a pattern of related descriptions of these unknown beings exists.

Among the Micmac, a group located in New Brunswick and Nova Scotia, are references to the *Gugwes*. "These cannibals have big hands and faces hairy like bears. If one saw a man coming he would lie down and beat his chest, producing a sound like a partridge" (Parsons 1925, p.56). Although the connection between a primate lying down and making a sound is unclear, this theme, the one-tone whistle (which is the call of the Gray Partridge, *Perdix perdix* of Southeastern Canada [Robbins et al. 1966]), is repeated in other areas as an item of these beings' behavior. The beasts are known by other Micmac names: *Kookwes, Chenoo, Djenu* (Wallis and Wallis 1955).

In Maine among the Penobscot, tales are told of *Kiwakwe*, a cannibal giant (Speck 1935b, p.81). Giants are familiar beings known, also, to the Huron and Wyandot as *Strendu*. They are half-a-tree tall and large in proportion to men. Furthermore, they are cannibals and covered with flinty scales. Their fate is unknown, but the belief is they are still living, perhaps east of the Lake Huron area where these tribes live (Barbeau 1914).

These beings seem very similar to those of upper New York State. Thus, the Stone Giants are huge men "covered" with flint and other stones.

> The Iroquoian Stone Giants, as well as their congeners among the Algonquians (e.g. the Chenoo of the Abnaki and Micmac), belong to a widespread group of mythic beings of which the Eskimo Tornit are examples. They are . . . huge in stature, unacquainted with the bow, and employing stones for weapons. In awesome combats they fight one another, uprooting the tallest trees for weapons and rending the earth in fury. . . . Commonly they are depicted as cannibals; and it may well be that this far-remembered mythic people is a reminiscence, coloured by time, of backward tribes of historic times. Of course, if there be such an historical element in these myths, it is coloured and overlaid by wholly mythic conceptions of stone-armoured Titans and demiurges (Alexander 1964, p. 29).

These ogres are the same as the *Windigo* (or *Witiko, Wendigo, Wittiko,* and other forms) of Algonkian origin. This extensive tradition covers eastern and central Canada and is well documented. Among the Tete-de-Boule of Quebec, this giant cannibalistic man is given different names: *Witiko, Kokotshe, Atshen* (Guinard 1930). The Micmac *Chenoo* appears to be similar with the Cree *Witiko*, for Cooper (1933, p. 23) states: "Both have the same characteristics . . . The very name Chenoo seems to be identical with the Montagnais and Tete-de-Boule (Cree) name, *Atcen*, for the Witiko." For also among the Naskapi "the nearest analogy in name and character with *Atcen* among neighboring peoples is the *Chenoo* (*Tcenu*) of Micmac legend" (Speck 1935a, p. 72).

Likewise specific traits clearly resemble those of parallel creatures in other areas.

> The witiko wore no clothes. Summer and winter he went naked and never suffered cold. His skin was black like that of a negro. He used to rub himself, like the animals, against fir, spruce, and other resinous trees. When he was thus covered

with gum or resin, he would go and roll in the sand, so that one would have thought that, after many operations of this kind, he was made of stone (Guinard 1930, p. 69).

Cooper (1933, p. 23) notes that

. . . a similar habit is ascribed to the Passamaquoddy Chenoo who used to rub themselves all over with fir balsam and then roll themselves on the ground so that everything adhered to the body.

This habit is highly suggestive of the Iroquoian Stone Coats, the blood-thirsty cannibal giants, who used to cover their bodies carefully with pitch and then roll and wallow in sand and down sand banks.

*Windigos* have a frightful and menacing mouth with no lips. Often a sinister hissing is made by them, or a noise, described as strident, very reverberating, and drawn out, is accompanied by fearful howls. *Windigo* is a huge individual "who goes naked in the bush and eats Indians. Many people claim to have heard him prowling in the woods" (Davidson 1928b, p.267). In Quebec, the Grand Lake Victoria Band relate tales of the *Misabe*, a giant with long hair (Davidson 1928a). Among the Ojibwa of northern Minnesota, Coleman (1937, p.41) describes "the *Memegwicio*, or men of the wilderness. Some called them a 'kind of monkey.' . . . And were described as being about the size of children of ten or eleven years of age . . . faces covered with hair." They appear to be a miniature *Windigo* and may, in fact, be the natives' attempt to categorize the young of the *Windigo.* Among the Tingami Ojibwa the *Memegwesi* are "a species of creature which lives in high remote ledges. They are small and have hair growing all over their bodies. The Indians think they are like monkeys judging from specimens of the latter they have seen in picture-books" (Speck 1915a, p. 82). Around James Bay, the Cree knew of the *memegwecio*, "the diminuitive being who looks like a human except that he is covered with hair and has a very flat nose" (Flannery 1946, p. 269). The general theme of hair (or the embellishment of sand and stone attached to it) gives these beasts, as well as all *Windigo*-type creatures, an unhumanlike quality. Indeed, from Micmac information Wallis and Wallis tell that the "Gugwes is a grotesque creature; in 1911-1912 he was commonly compared to a baboon; in 1950 he was described as a giant" (1955, p. 417).

Among the Northern Athabascan Indians in the Canadian plains and Alaska, a concept persists of the *Nakani*, human figures living in the bush country. They are also referred to as "Bad Indians," Brush-men, and by similar names. Detailed descriptions of them are lacking both from disbelief by chroniclers and because the *Nakani* reputedly depart when still at a distance from any observer. These beings are said to be active only in the summer foliage, spending winters underground in camouflaged pit lodges. Their presence is often known by whistling heard in the woods or by the observation of shoe-like tracks. In the past, they were known to travel in groups, but presently they are observed only singly.

In the early 1960s, VanStone (1965, p.105) notes this belief in the *Nakani* among the Chipewyan at the settlement of Snowdrift on Great Slave Lake:

> There is also much discussion among the Snowdrift Indians concerning so-called "bush men" who are believed to roam the bush during the summer months, frequently coming near the village. They are sometimes used as a device to frighten children. . . . However, adults believe in them too, and several people told the author of encounters with "bushmen."

During the previous century at nearby Fort Resolution, Ross (1872, p. 309) observes among the Indians their fear of "enemies." He relates that "I have on several occasions caused all the natives encamped around to flock for protection into the fort during the night by simply whistling, hidden in the bushes."

MacNeish (1954, pp.185-188) and Osgood (1932, pp.85-86) describe the characteristics and stories of the *Nakani* among the tribes in the area of Great Bear Lake. Further to the west, the presence of this belief is well documented among the Kutchin in the northern Yukon and Alaska (Osgood 1936, pp.154, 157; and Slobodin 1960, pp.126-129) and on the Kenai Peninsula (Osgood 1937, pp.171-173). Typically these beings are recounted to kidnap women and children. Attitudes toward these creatures seem to reflect recent events attributed to encounters with them in that disappearances and alleged attacks create apprehension in some areas, especially for women and children.

The origin of this widespread and consistent belief remains an unsettled question. One clearly expressed and relevant observation of this belief is made by MacNeish (1954, p.186), Osgood (1937, p.171), and VanStone (1965, p.105). They state that the *Nakani* have no supernatural powers and are human figures with characteristics and habits that set them apart from ordinary humans.

The "stone" theme reappears among the Shoshonean tales. Of these beings "the northern Shoshoni say that formerly there were numerous Stone Giants (Dzoavits) dwelling in the hills" (Alexander 1964, p.134). Although no information is given as to the nature of the "stone" of these giants, the same evolution, from hairy covering to some type of resin or gum base with sand attached, most probably occurred here as with those recorded in the East.

From the northern interior of British Columbia, among the Kaska Indians, are told the stories of men with coarse, thick hair (Teit 1917). Another Athabascan group, the Sinkoyne, have tales of men who are somewhat bear-like (Gifford 1937). The Anderson and Seton Lake Indians of British Columbia tell of numerous giants (Elliot 1931). As can be seen, this tradition comes to its highest embodiment in British Columbia. For example, among the Carrier, one of these monsters "left enormous footprints in the snow. . . . It had the face of a human being, it was exceedingly tall . . . and covered with long hair" (Jenness 1934, p. 221). A similar tradition is common in the Lillooet. The beings, called *Hailō Laux* or *Haitló laux,* are very tall people, men that are ten feet tall and broad and strong. They have hair on their breasts and look like bears. The hair on the head is long. Most of them are black-haired, some brown, but quite a number do have red hair. The Indians believe they are bad people, wander about at night, and are never known to sleep (Teit 1912). The last idiosyncrasy may refer to the beast's natural nocturnal foraging. Among the Karok and Yurok, as Kroeber (1925, p.304) observes, there is the sharp impression "of the idea of an ancient prehuman but parallel race." This same belief seems to be prevalent throughout the Northwest today via Bigfoot and Sasquatch accounts (Sanderson 1961; Green 1969; Patterson 1966).

Although the present day encounters in the Pacific Northwest are almost something of an everyday occurrence, another living tradition does exist in the East. The accounts from Monroe, Michigan, are well known, and need not be recounted in detail here. What is noteworthy is the chronology of events before and after the major Monroe sightings. On August 9, 1965, east of Smithville, Ontario, a Lakeview truck driver reported seeing a seven-foot-tall, hairy beast with broad shoulders, a small head, and long arms, near the side of a back road. Near Monroe, Michigan, on August 13, a seven-foot-tall something with hairs "like quills" reached through an automobile window, and gave Christine Van Acker a now famous blackened left eye. Other "sightings" were made thereafter around Monroe. One of the most extraordinary in the eyes of the local authorities was the claim of two fishermen on Voorheis Lake, Oakland County, who stated they had seen an amphibious creature emerge from the lake. Then in early September of 1965, came reports of a monster prowling around Tillsonburg, Ontario. Its footprints were plainly visible (in sand) and measured 18 inches in length.* Thus a traveling "Windigo," if you will, appears to have come by Smithville on its way to Michigan, and returned via Tillsonburg. Sketchy reports from Newmarket, Ontario, for 1965, may be but another leg in this beast's route. Could the cool nature of the summer of 1965, the coolest since 1950, have forced the movement of a lone ABSM into the habitat of man? Perhaps, but the record shows the August-September, 1965, reports are only outstanding because of their correlation in time and space. The Fremont, Wisconsin, (November 1968) case is known to most, but ABSM-people encounters also took place that year in Easterville, Manitoba, and La Crescent, Minnesota. In June of 1964, at Sister Lakes, Michigan, [it] "happened," but this would

*The provincial police "explained away" these by coming to the conclusion that the tracks were made by "a tired tobacco worker crawling on his hands and knees between the tobacco rows." (*Kitchener-Waterloo Record*, Saturday, September 4, 1965.) By Fort, they certainly can come up with some wonderful explanations!

have been of little surprise to Phillip Williams and Otto Collins who were picked up and carried for a short distance by an ape-like thing with a rotten smell near Marshall, Michigan, in May of 1956.

The basis of the aboriginal traditions may seem hazy to the folklorist and anthropologist, but as for the people who have come face to face with a member of the population of Bigfoot/Sasquatches of the Pacific Northwest or with an individual of the similar remnant race of the East, one doubts if you could convince these observers of the worthless validity of subhominid tales.

*References*

Alexander, Hartley Burr. 1964. *North American*, vol. X of *Mythology of All Races*. L.H. Gray, ed. 13 vols. New York:Cooper Square Pub., Inc.

Barbeau, C. M. 1914. "Supernatural Beings of the Huron and Wyandot." *American Anthropologist* 16: 288–313.

Berton, Pierre. 1956. *The Mysterious North*. New York: Alfred A. Knopf.

Boas, Franz. 1897. "Traditions of the Ts' ets' a ut." *Journal of American Folklore* 10: 35–48.

––––––. 1964. *The Central Eskimo*. Lincoln, Neb.: Univ. of Nebraska Press.

Bogoras, Wladimar. 1902. "The Folklore of Northeastern Asia as Compared with That of Northwestern America." *American Antropologist* 4: 577–684.

Coleman, Sister Bernard. 1937. "The Religion of the Ojibwa of Northern Minnesota." *Primitive Man* 10:41.

Cooper, John M. 1933. "The Cree Witiko Psychosis." *Primitive Man* 6: 20–24.

Davidson, D. S. 1928a. "Folktales from Grand Lake Victoria, Quebec." *Journal of American Folklore* 41: 275.

––––––. 1928b. "Some Tete De Boule." *Journal of American Folklore* 41: 267.

Elliot, W. C. 1931. "Lake Lillooet Tales." *Journal of American Folklore* 43: 174.

Flannery, Regina. 1946. "The Culture of Northeastern Indians." In *Man in Northeastern North America*, ed., Johnson. (Papers of the Robert S. Peabody Foundation for Archaeology, Vol. 3.) Andover, Mass.: Phillips Acad.

Gifford, E. W. 1937. "Coast Yuki Tales." *Journal of American Folklore* 50: 142.

Green, John W. 1969. *On the Track of the Sasquatch.* Agassiz, British Columbia: Cheam Publishing, Ltd.

Guinard, Rev. Joseph E. 1930. "Witiko among the Tete-de-Boule." *Primitive Man* 3: 69–71.

Jenness, Diamond. 1934. "Myths of the Carrier Indians of British Columbia." *Journal of American Folklore* 47.

Kroeber, Alfred L. 1899. "Tales of Smith Sound Eskomos." *Journal of American Folklore* 12: 166–167.

———. 1925. *Handbook of the Indians of California.* Bureau of American Ethnology, Bulletin 78.

MacNeish, June Helm. 1954. "Contemporary Folk Beliefs of a Slave Indian Band." *Journal of American Folklore* 67: 185–198.

Osgood, Cornelius B. 1932. "The Ethnography of the Great Bear Lake Indians." Ottawa: National Museum of Canada, Bulletin 70 (Annual Report for 1931).

———. 1936. "Contributions to the Ethnography of the Kutchin." Yale Univ. Pub. in Anthropology, No. 14.

———. 1937. "The Ethnography of the Tanaina." Yale Univ. Pub. in Anthropology, No. 16.

Parsons, Elsie Clews. 1925. "Tales of the Micmac." *Journal of American Folklore* 38: 56.

Patterson, Roger. 1966. *Do Abominable Snowmen of America Really Exist?* Yakima, Washington: Franklin Press, Inc.

Robbins, Chandler S., Brunn, B., and Zim, H. S. 1966. *Birds of North America.* New York: Golden Press.

Ross, Bernard R. 1872. "The Eastern Tinneh." Washington, D.C.: Annual Report to the Board of Regents of the Smithsonian Inst. (1866).

Sanderson, Ivan T. 1961. *Abominable Snowmen: Legend Come to Life.* Philadelphia: Chilton Co.

Scherman, Katherine. 1956. *Spring on an Arctic Island.* Boston: Little, Brown, and Co.

Slobodin, Richard. 1960. "Some Social Functions of Kutchin Anxiety." *American Anthropologist* 62: 122–133.

Speck, Frank G. 1915. *Myths and Folklore of the Timiskaming Algonquin and Timagami Ojibwa.* Anthropological Series, Canada Dept. of Mines, Geological Survey, No. 9.

———. 1935*a. Naskapi.* Norman: University of Oklahoma.

———. 1935*b.* "Tales of the Penobscot." *Journal of American Folklore* 48: 81.

Spencer, Robert F. 1959. *The North Alaskan Eskimo.* Bureau of American Ethnology, Bulletin 71.

Teit, James. 1912. "Traditions of the Lillooet Indians of British Columbia." *Journal of American Folklore* 25: 346–347.

———. 1917. "Kaska Tales." *Journal of American Folklore* 30: 438.

VanStone, James W. 1965. "The Changing Culture of the Snowdrift Chipewyan." Bulletin 209. Ottawa: National Museum of Canada.

Wallis, Wilson D., and Wallis, Ruth Sawtell. 1955. *The Micmac Indians of Eastern Canada.* Minneapolis: Univ. of Minnesota Press.

*Concerning the abominable men of America, a little-known occurrence in nineteenth-century Arkansas is mentioned by Otto Ernest Rayburn in his* Ozark Country *(New York: Duell, Sloan & Pearce, 1941).*

An interesting story from the Ouachita Mountains is the one about the Giant of the Mountains. This wild man, more than six and one-half feet tall, was seen many times in the remote mountains of Saline County during the years after the Civil War. He was a white man, wore no clothes, and his body was covered with long, thick hair. Most of the time he lived in caves, but he was sometimes seen in the tall reeds on the banks of the Saline River. Although no one had ever seen him harm anyone, the giant was exceedingly feared by all the colonists for miles around, and they fled from him as from the devil. He had never been heard to utter a sound, and this enhanced his mysteriousness. Ultimately it was decided that he had to be captured, and an expedition was organized for this hunt. An audacious young man took charge of it with a pack of hunting dogs. The wild man was tracked to a cave and lassoed. When the ring of the lasso fell on his shoulders, he made a strange sound like that of an animal caught in a trap. He was led to Benton and lodged in the prison, which was a small log cabin. He immediately tore off the clothes placed on him by his captors, and escaped from his fragile prison, but was re-captured, this time in the reeds.

Exactly what became of this wild man no one seems to know. The old people of the country say he disappeared and was never again seen in the area. The following story is a sequel.

Shortly after the giant's escape, the young man who had led the first hunt rushed into his parents' cabin, seized his rifle, and cried to his mother, "Ma, don't look for me until you see me coming. I'll be gone maybe for a day, or maybe for a year." He had found huge footprints and wanted to follow them while the trail was fresh.

These footprints were 13⅔ inches long and four feet apart. The place was located, as we said before, in Saline County, not far from Benton, the County seat. According to this story, the young man succeeded in following these tracks across southern Arkansas and as far as Texas. Along the way he met nine other men who had found and where following the enormous footprints. In their company he crossed Texas, eating almost nothing but raw meat killed along the way.

Almost a year passed before the young man returned to Arkansas with the disappointing news that not one of those following the trail had seen the giant who was leaving these tracks, although they had met several people who said they had seen him, always moving about in the darkness of the night.

*The notes and documents of the late Mr. Rayburn are now in* the collections of the University of Arkansas in Fayetteville (under the collective title Encyclopedia of Ozark Folklore). In a letter of May 18, 1966, Marvin A. Miller, Director of Libraries for the University of Arkansas, wrote that, "We have checked the possible articles in Rayburn's Encyclopedia of Ozark Folklore, and have found no references to the 'Giant of the Mountains.' "

It would be interesting to learn more about the basis for Mr. Rayburn's story.

\* \* \*

Another "monster" is supposed to have appeared more recently in Cass County, Michigan, not far from Detroit, in a sparsely populated region. True magazine for June 1966 contained an article entitled, "The Mad Hunt for the Monster of Michigan," by Gene Caesar, which gives a good idea of the best way in which not to find a "monster." The Michigan creature was also mentioned in the highly respected New York Times for August 17, 1966, and even by NBC Television (on the "Huntley-Brinkley Report") on the same day.

\* \* \*

The hunt for the abominable snowman of America, the Sasquatch, the Bigfoot, etc., is constantly continuing, but it seems that there now exists a short film of a female Bigfoot. On October 20, 1967, Roger Patterson, a member of an advance research group from Yakima, Washington, took some thirty feet of film in northern California, the positives of which show a large humanoid creature (approximately six to six and one-half feet tall), covered with shining black hair, and having prominent buttocks and a kind of "crest" on its head.

As could have been anticipated, this film gave rise to controversy. Some scientists have rejected, but many others have accepted subject to examination, the idea that there could really be something there in these wild regions and that biologists should determine exactly what. Ivan T. Sanderson, who is recognized as the top specialist in this field, considers the film genuine. He has *devoted serious study to the problem for many years, and has written the most complete work in existence on the subject,* Abominable Snowmen: Legend Come to Life *(Philadelphia: Chilton Co., 1961).*

*Dr. John Napier, a member of the Primate Biology Program of the Smithsonian Institution in Washington, says he "has seen nothing which on the scientific level would be indicative of a hoax." Dr. Osman Hill of the Yerkes Regional Center for Primate Research, Emory University in Atlanta, Georgia, feels strongly that additional studies should be made with complete objectivity.*

*George Haas of San Francisco is another tireless investigator of rumors of the Bigfoot in the United States and northwestern Canada. In a letter, he mentions a report concerning a Bigfoot killed in British Columbia in the fall of 1967, and whose body remained covered by snow throughout the winter. Rapid and thorough follow-up and examination of this matter would have been very interesting.*

## In Search of the Abominable Snowman in the Rockies

*From* La Presse, *Montréal, Canada, for September 2, 1969*

Nordegg, Alberta (PC)—Many citizens of this region are convinced that a band of hairy creatures, of humanoid type, lives in the nearby Rockies.

A merchant of this town—situated 120 miles southeast [sic—actually southwest!] of Edmonton—has the intention of setting out on an expedition which will seek the "Abominable Snowman of the Pacific."

"So many people have seen them, and we found so many tracks that I am convinced that there is something there," disclosed this citizen in an interview at the end of the week.

*Five eyewitnesses*

The most recent eyewitnesses of these anthropoids are five men

Figure 6. Artist's conception of the large anthropoid seen in the Canadian Rockies near Nordegg, Alberta. From *La Presse*, Montreal, September 2, 1969.

who are working on a vast builders yard at Big Horn Dam, on the North Saskatchewan river. According to one of the witnesses, Mr. Floyd Engen, of Eckville, Alberta, the creature measures some 15 feet and is of a dark color, probably because of his hair, and has sloping shoulders.

The chief editor of the *Agassiz Weekly* in British Columbia,

Mr. John Green, thinks that this anthropoid is a Sasquatch, weighing five tons.

Many people, including Indians, scientists, workers, technicians have given descriptions which correspond to the same description of this kind of Yeti, which walks with giant steps.

## A Sasquatch Expert Sure of Sighting

*From the* Vancouver Sun *for August 2, 1969*

Agassiz—British Columbia's best-known Sasquatch hunter is convinced the latest sighting in Washington state was a true Sasquatch.

"There is no doubt about it being real," said John Green, publisher and editor of the *Agassiz Advance*. Green returned Friday from a one-day trip to Grays Harbor, Washington, where a deputy sheriff reported seeing a mysterious beast. Green said he does not have time to pursue the hunt but is encouraging other Sasquatch buffs to go into the heavily-wooded area.

The deputy, whose identity has not been released, told Green he saw the animal in the middle of the road at 2:35 A.M., while returning home from work. He said the animal was not a bear. It had no snout, and its face had a leathery look.

It was 7 to 7½ feet tall, and weighed about 300 to 325 pounds, he said. It had hands with fingers, and feet with toes.

The deputy told Green he photographed one track at the edge of the road and it measured about 18½ inches long. The animal walked upright.

(Later the sheriff at Grays Harbor said the unidentified deputy was now convinced it was a bear.)

## A Sasquatch Seen in the United States?

*From the* Herald *of Calgary, Alberta, Canada, for July 31, 1969*

Hoquiam, Washington (AP)—A part-time sheriff's deputy,

who describes himself as "solid," says he saw an eight-foot creature with a human-like face in the woods near here, fitting the description of the legendary Sasquatch.

The Sasquatch is a fabled man-like ape of Indian legend on the West Coast, something like the better-known Abominable Snowman of the Himalayas.

The deputy, who declined use of his name, said the creature weighed about 300 pounds, had hairless feet and hands, "and a human-like face." He said it was something like a bear.

"It's a hard position to be in," he said, "because people say you're nuts."

## Strange "Men" Sighted

*From the* Chicago Tribune *for July 23, 1969*

Rangoon, Burma, July 22 (Reuters)—Burmese officials are studying reports claiming that two creatures twice the height of an average man and covered with dark brown hair were sighted along Burma's western border on the Mekong River.

## Search Planned for "Hairy Men"

*From the* Vancouver Sun *for August 7, 1969*

Kuala Lumpur, Malaysia (UPI)—The son of the Sultan of Pahang will lead an expedition in search of the mysterious "hairy creatures" reported to have been sighted in the jungles of Pahang State 160 miles east of Kuala Lumpur.

Rattan cutters and loggers who claim to have seen the creatures say they look like a cross between apes and humans.

They were about four feet tall and the females were fairer and had longer hair than the males, they said.

The department of aborigine affairs, after studying the footprints left behind by the creatures, said it believed that they were those of the Orang Batik (Batik people), a very shy primitive tribe.

The sultan's son, Tengku Mahkota, said: "This is something I would like to see for myself. I intend to go into the jungles with a party as soon as fresh reports are received."

## The Malaysian Army Alerted
## A "Giant" Frightens the Town of Segamat

*From the* Diario de Las Palmas, *Canary Islands, for August 9, 1966*

The Malaysian Territorial Army has received orders to be alert and to shoot on sight a "giant" which has frightened the town of Segamat, situated 160 kilometers to the southwest of the capital, according to a story in the "Utusan Melayu."

In this story the so-called "giant" gave a good scare to several soldiers in their camp. One of the men said that he heard steps when he was on guard duty at night, and in the light of a bonfire, saw a monster six meters tall [over 18 feet!]. The "giant" disappeared immediately on being seen by the sentinel.

The inhabitants of the state of Kampong Bangis, 15 kilometers from Segamat, reported last week that they encountered footprints 45 cm. [18 inches] long, 15 cm. [six inches] wide, and 12.5 cm. [5 inches] deep in the earth.

A guard at a game preserve stated that the "giant" caused no danger to anyone.

# ARE THERE STILL DINOSAURS?

## Ivan T. Sanderson

*Three men, the Belgian Bernard Heuvelmans, the Russian Boris Porchnev, and the American Ivan T. Sanderson, have in recent years created and are still developing a strange science— crypto-zoology—the search for animals whose existence established zoology does not wish to acknowledge.*

*The article reprinted here is a historical event. In its original form, it dates from 1948, and at that time it created something of a scandal. Sanderson, a zoologist of note, retracted none of it in 1972.*

*Since that time, other facts have been collected that seem to prove his thesis.*

*It seems clear that there exist on land and in the oceans gigantic creatures that may be living fossils, unless they are the product of relatively recent mutations and recall the forms of the past only by virtue of laws of evolutionary convergence as yet unknown to us.*

*Science may have much to learn from these apparitions that seem to have come out of science fiction.*

There is a very curious business going on in Africa that merits careful consideration and a good airing. The mere thought of it is an abomination to scientists, but it is a matter that nevers fails to excite our imagination. It revolves around the question, doubtless born of wishful thinking, that all of us have probably at one time or another asked ourselves—namely, could there be a few dinosaurs still living in the remoter corners of the earth?

We really have nothing but negative evidence to warrant our stating that the dinosaurs are extinct, while, astonishing as it may seem, there are apparently quite a few people who actually believe that they still exist. The evidence they present, moreover, is positive, though even they cannot deny that it is purely circumstantial. Much of it may probably and quite justifiably be disposed of as wishful thinking, as examples of mistaken identity, scientific overenthusiasm, native stupidity or even bad liquor; but there are some things like the tuatara, a two-foot lizard-shaped creature from New Zealand, and some millions of crocodiles that cannot be gainsaid, for they are just as real as the elephants in our zoos and the cattle in our fields. All the facts, moreover, are on record, so let us examine them, beginning with what will probably be regarded as the lunatic fringe.

A well-known South African big-game hunter, delighting in the name of Mr. F. Gobler, returned from a trip to Angola and announced to the Capetown newspaper, the *Cape Argus*, that there was an animal of large dimensions, the description of which could only fit a dinosaur, dwelling in the Dilolo Swamps, and well known to the natives as the *chipekwe*. He stated: "Its weight would be about four tons and it attacks rhino, hippo and elephants. Hunters have heard a *chipekwe*—at night—devouring a dead rhino, crushing the bones and tearing out huge lumps of meat. It has the head and tail of a lizard. A German scientist has photographed it. I went to the swamps in search of it, but the natives told me it was extremely rare, and I could not locate the monster. Nevertheless I am convinced the *chipekwe* does exist. Here is the photograph."

This, of course, produced a terrific outburst in the editorial and correspondence columns of the paper, but the astonishing thing is that the majority of the experts, both scientific and sporting, and all with much local knowledge, agreed that it might exist. Their reasons will become abundantly clear later.

I doubt if any of us would believe such a tale, even if related in all solemnity by the most renowned explorer, and yet a well-known big-game hunter named Maj. H. C. Maydon, with over a decade of experience chasing animals in Africa, has written of this and a number of similar statements: "Do I believe them? Of course; why not? I add fifty percent for native exaggeration, but I believe there is more than 'something' in them. I met a man, an old hunter-prospector, once in Livingstone, Rhodesia, who swore that he had seen a water monster in Lake Mweru and had studied its tracks. Why has no one yet seen these beasts in the flesh for certain or brought one to bag? Because they are forest or swamp dwellers. How many people have seen a bongo or a giant forest hog or a yellow-backed duiker, and yet they are not excessively rare."

Worse than this, however, we have to face the fact that the greatest animal dealer of all time, Carl Hagenbeck, not only believed in such reports but actually invested a very considerable sum in an expedition which he sent out to Africa under his best professional collector to search for the creature. A hard-boiled businessman with many years' experience in buying and selling animals simply does not do such a thing unless he has very real grounds for expecting concrete returns on his money. Hegenbeck, moreover, had such grounds, which he states in his own words as follows: "I received reports from two quite distinct sources of the existence of an immense and wholly unknown animal said to inhabit the interior of Rhodesia. Almost identical stories reached me, firstly, through one of my own travelers and, secondly, through an English gentleman who had been shooting big game in Central

Africa. The reports were thus quite independent of each other. The natives, it seemed, had told both my informants that in the depths of the great swamps there dwelt a huge monster, half elephant, half dragon. This however, is not the only evidence for the existence of the animal. It is now several decades ago since Menges, who is, of course, perfectly reliable, heard a precisely similar story from the Negros; and, still more remarkable, on the walls of certain caverns in Central Africa there are to be found actual drawings of this strange creature. From what I have heard of the animal, it seems to me that it can only be some kind of dinosaur, seemingly akin to the brontosaurus."

Now it is easy enough to scoff at these tales and even to pity the sporting major and the poor, gullible animal dealer. It is quite permissible to treat such reports with a healthy skepticism and it is assuredly prudent to do so, unless you want to have the entire fraternity of zoologists on your neck. Nonetheless, to let the matter rest there would be utterly unscientific. The very basis of science is a healthy skepticism—one, moreover, that should question the skeptic who denies the possibility of anything just as readily as the benighted traveler who dares to affirm it.

The borderland of zoology is very extensive; the number of animals still to be discovered on this small planet is much greater than is popularly realized or science is prepared to advertise. Nor are all of these microscopic worms or tiny, obscure tropical beetles, for a large and perfectly distinct species of cheetah, taller than a leopard, turned up in a fairly well-known part of East Africa only a few years ago; and the famous case of the okapi, an animal as large as a horse that was only a rumor until 1900, is now well known. The number of entirely new types of animals that are discovered every year is amazing.

This brings us to the next set of facts which anybody with a truly unbiased mind should contemplate.

A notion has somehow gained popular credence that the surface of the earth is now fully explored and for the most part well known and even mapped. There was never a greater misconception. The percentage of the land surface of the earth that is actually inhabited—that is to say, lived upon, enclosed, farmed or regularly traversed—is quite limited. Even if the territory that is penetrated only for hunting or the gathering of food crops be added, vast areas still remain completely unused.

There are such areas in every continent, areas that are never even so much as entered for years on end by any man. Nor are these only the hot deserts of the torrid regions or the cold deserts of the poles. I have visited a house in New Jersey behind which the woods extend in one direction, unbroken by so much as a path, for twenty-one miles.

In parts of the tropics there are areas of quite staggering immensity which no man has as yet been able to penetrate. Whole mountain ranges in Australia have never even been seen from the ground; large parts of the northern Himalayas are as yet unvisited; regions of New Guinea have never been reached; and considerable portions of the Amazon valley are quite unknown. The Addar swamps in Central Africa cover 1800 square miles, those of the Bahr el Ghazal several thousands, and parts of them cannot be traversed. Just because a map is covered with names does not mean that the country is known. Aerial surveys with modern photographic technique only add to the popular misconception, for lots of physical features are recorded in some detail and rapidly find their way into our atlases. These are given names and fill up the space, but all the time the country remains absolutely untouched.

The notion, therefore, that any beast could not exist either because of its size or because somebody would sooner or later have seen it, is really quite absurd. There might easily be creatures as big as elephants living in some profusion in, say, the back of Dutch Guiana, which is now only seventeen hours' flight in a commercial plane from Miami.*

Such animals might have been well known to several thousand people for hundreds of years, but their presence would still be unsuspected by us, for none of the Amerindians who, from aerial surveys, are known to exist in that area, has ever come out or even been seen by anybody from outside.

*Today the same flight would only take three hours—R. J. Willis.

Another fact that is often not sufficiently appreciated even by experts is the extraordinary selectivity displayed by many animals in choosing their places of abode. Larger animals especially tend to stay within a most limited area that is often very distinctive as far as vegetation and other environmental conditions are concerned. Even nomadic creatures often travel only from one patch of some particular kind of forest to another of the same, and avoid all other kinds as they would a forest fire. Hippopotamus will abound in certain stretches of a river and never be seen in others.

This trait often accounts for the supposed rarity of many animals, when in point of fact and apart from species that are actually on the road to rapid extinction, there is probably no such thing as a rare animal. It is merely a question of finding where it lives and how it lives, and in that place it will prove to be quite common. Any creature living in a tropical swamp surrounded by dry jungles would always stay there and, if that swamp could not be penetrated by man, might never be seen. In such a swamp of two thousand square miles' extent, many very large beasts could lurk.

The possibilities become even greater if the animals in question be semi-aquatic, and it is interesting to note in this connection that all the accounts of as yet unidentified beasts which sound like dinosaurs are of swamp creatures that retreat into the water when alarmed.

The vastness of Africa is a byword and can be attested by thousands of our wartime fliers, but to be really appreciated it has to be seen from the ground. Also it is only on the ground that one comes to understand the true nature of the tropical forests and swamplands. A companion and I once spent a full five minutes peering into quite a small patch of bushes trying to see an animal apparently about as bulky as the two of us put together, that we could actually hear breathing. We never did see it, even when it took fright and left, making about as much noise as a light tank. On another occasion I was in a canoe among reeds in Africa and, after looking up at the sun ahead to take my bearings, bent down to pick up a cigarette. When I looked up again there was a full-grown bull elephant almost on top of me. As I watched, quivering, it sank down behind the reeds, and although I immediately stood up in the canoe so that I could almost see over the swamp, I never even heard the vast beast again, nor did I see so much as a single reed move.

This was only a mile from a native village of two thousand souls and in an area where elephants had not, as far as I could learn, been seen within living memory.

Small wonder, then, that residents of Africa, and especially those who have hunted big game in more distant parts, do not readily scoff at these tales which provoke us to so much laughter—tales such as that brought out of the Congo by a certain Monsieur Lepage in 1920.

This man returned from a hunting trip and announced that he had come upon an extraordinary animal of great size in a swamp. It had charged him, making a snorting noise, and he had fired wildly but, seeing that it did not halt, he had retreated precipitately. When the monster abandoned the chase he turned and examined it through a pair of binoculars for some considerable period. He stated that it was eight meters—about twenty-six feet—long, had a long pointed snout, a short horn above the nostrils and a scaly hump on its shoulders. The forefeet appeared to be solid, like those of a horse, but the hindfeet were separated into digits.

The most astonishing thing about these reports, however, is not so much their prevalence as the widespread points of their origin, Here again our modern atlases are very misleading because the practice—born quite properly of necessity—of squeezing the whole of Africa onto one page gives the impression that the Cameroons are not really very far from the Upper Nile. This distance is actually 1600 miles, and the territory in between is a vast land of forests, swamps and savannahs. The natives on one side have no connection whatsoever with those on the other, and yet very similar stories are rife at both extremes.

These native tales are to be met with throughout the equatorial rain forest belt from Gambia in the west to the Nile in the east, and south to Angola and Rhodisia. Carl Hagenbeck's collectors picked them up in Liberia, and the leader of a German expedition to the Cameroons in 1913 made a very interesting report which has never been published in full, but which has been quoted by several others. In widely separated areas, he collected descriptions of an alleged beast named the *mokele-mbembe* from experienced native guides who could not possibly have known each other.

His description states: "The animal is said to be of a brownish-gray color with a smooth skin, its size approximating that of an elephant; at least that of a hippopotamus. It is said to have a long and very flexible neck and only one tooth but a very long one; *some say it is a horn*. A few spoke about a long muscular tail like that of an alligator.

"Canoes coming near it are said to be doomed; the animal is said to attack the vessels at once and to kill the crews, but without eating the bodies. The creature is said to live in the caves that have been washed out by the river in the clay of its shores at sharp bends. It is said to climb the shore even at daytime in search of food; its diet is said to be entirely vegetable. This feature disagrees with a possible explanation as a myth. The preferred plant was shown to me; it is a kind of liana with large white blossoms, with a milky sap and applelike fruits. At the Ssombo River I was shown a path said to have been made by this animal in order to get at its food. The path was fresh and there were plants of the described type near by. But since there were too many tracks of elephants, hippos, and other large mammals, it was impossible to make out a particular spoor with any amount of certainty."

This brings up the whole question of native tales, over which there is perhaps more acrimonious debate than over any other subject. Opinions appear to be about equally divided among those who have lived in Africa, but both parties tend to overlook certain facts. Because of his animistic beliefs, the African lives in a world peopled by a host of spirits which are nonetheless just as real to him as animals are to us, and he may describe these with great clarity of expression.

However, we must at the same time place against this the African's customary and remarkable knowledge of natural history and the fact that usually he not only has a name for all the animals in his country but also knows their habits and their slightest variations in great detail.

The African can, however, develop a maddening habit of exaggeration or even outright fabrication if he desires to please an inquiring foreigner. Against this, in turn, must be placed his very widespread reluctance to publicize anything in his territory that might conceivably be of value to the outsider lest, as he has learned from unhappy experience, a new tax immediately be clapped upon it. If you do get a tribal African's confidence and he starts to talk about animals, as opposed to the spirit creatures of his country, it is well worth while to listen intently, for it must not be forgotten that certain Africans always contended that mosquitoes had something to do with malaria, a fact we proved only quite recently. Others similarly talked about the okapi for a very long time before it was actually shot be a white man.

Sometimes the African's patience with us and our disbelief of things he knows well becomes exhausted, and even he resorts to the writing of official minutes.

The now famous report of the late King Lewanika, of the Barotse tribe, is of this nature. The king, who took great interest in the fauna of his country, constantly heard of a large reptile that lived in the great swamps. He had passed this information on, but, since nobody believed it, he gave strict orders that the next time any of his people saw the animal they were immediately to tell him. After some time three men did so report, saying that they had come across the beast at the edge of a marsh, that it had a long neck and small, snakelike head and that it had retreated into the swamp on its belly. King Lewanika immediately visited the spot and states in his official minutes that it had left a track in the reeds "as large as a full-sized wagon would make were its wheels removed."

Other native evidence comes from widely separated sources. An experienced white hunter named Stephens, who was also in charge of a long section of the telegraph line which runs along the banks of the Upper Nile, has given a great deal of information about a large, swamp-dwelling reptile known to a number of tribes as the *lau*. The natives described the animal to Stephens in great detail and more than one of them affirmed that they had been present at the killing of a *lau*. They variously described it as being between forty and a hundred feet long, but concurred in stating that the body was as big as a donkey, that it was dark yellow in color and that it had a vicious, snake-like head, with large tentacles or wiry hairs with which it reached out to seize its prey. Later a Belgian administrator from the Congo asserted that he had seen a *lau* several times in a swamp and had shot at it.

The most convincing native account, however, comes from Northern Rhodesia. This seems to be of an animal more akin to the *chipekwe*, and an Englishman who spent eighteen years on Lake Bengweulu in that country has given an account of the slaying of one, as described by the local chief, who had it from his grand-father. Apparently the tribesmen had killed the creature with the hippo spears. It had a smooth, hairless, dark body and the head was adorned with a single white ivory horn. The story was firmly rooted in local tradition, and the Englishman in question believed in the existence of the animal, for he reports that a retired local administrator had heard some very large animal splashing in a lake in the nighttime and had the next morning examined large unknown spoor on the bank.

The mention of a single ivory horn brings us to a whole set of most interesting facts that were assembled from quite another source. Some years ago the excavation of the famous Ishtar Gate of Babylon by the German professor, Robert Koldewey, brought to light a number of startlingly realistic bas-reliefs of a dragonlike animal with curiously mixed features. It had a scaled body, long tail and neck, hindfeet of a bird and forefeet of a lion and a strange reptilian head sporting a single straight, upright horn like that of a rhinoceros, wrinkles under its neck, a crest like a modern iguana lizard, and a very pronounced, serpentine tongue. At first this fabulous creature was classed along with the winged, human-headed bulls and other fabulous monsters of Babylonian mythol-ogy, but profound researches gradually forced the professor to quite a different conclusion.

The creature had the name of the *sirrush* and the priests were said to have held it in a dark cavern in the temple. It was depicted on the walls of the Ishtar Gate in great numbers and in association with a large, oxlike animal which is now known to have been the extinct aurochs and very definitely a real animal.

When analyzed, allowing for some considerable Babylonian artistic license, the strangely mixed characters of the *sirrush* appeared to be much less fabulous than had at first been supposed, and, despite his solid Teutonic background, Professor Koldewey became more and more convinced that it was not a representation of a mythical creature but an attempt to depict a real animal, an example or examples of which had actually been kept alive in Babylon in very early days by the priests.

After much searching in the depths of his cautious scientific soul, he even made so bold as to state in print that this animal was one of the plant-eating, bird-footed dinosaurs, many types of which had by that time been reconstructed from fossil remains. He further pointed out that such remains were not to be found anywhere in or near Mesopotamia and that the sirrush could not be a Babylonian attempt to reconstruct the animal from fossils. Its characters as shown in Babylonian art from the earliest times had not changed, and displayed great detail in scales, horns, wrinkles, the crest and the serpentine tongue, which, taken together could not all have been just thought up after viewing a fossilized skeleton.

On further analysis the *sirrush* seems to display characteristics of the *chipekwe* of Lake Bangweulu, of Monsieur Lepage's beast from the Congo, Carl Hagenbeck's half-elephant-half-dragon, and of the *mokele-mbembe*, and even of the *lau*. The single horn on the snout, the scaled hump on the shoulders, the solid forefeet and cloven hindfeet, the long neck and small serpentine head and even the tentacles of the *lau* all appear in the *sirrush*.

The final link, however, is that one of Carl Hagenbeck's collectors picked up in Central Africa, in the locality where the *chipekwe* tales are most prevalent, some glazed bricks of the exact type used in the construction of the Ishtar Gate, and which are, as far as we know, unique to that time and country. This is much less fabulous than it sounds, for there is absolute evidence that seaborne trade had been carried on even by the Sumerians before the rise of Babylon, between Mesopotamia and the east coast of Africa which was called Me-lukh-kha and was said to be inhabited by Salmuti, meaning "black men." If a horned, herbivorous, bird-footed dinosaur existed in Africa at that time, a captive specimen or specimens might well have been shipped back to Mesopotamia, where they would undoubtedly have created quite a stir and become the exclusive property of the ruling priesthood. Their presence as sacred beasts would prompt the making of very careful portraits on important monuments.

Whether the Babylonian *sirrush* and the other creatures rumored to have come from Africa exist now, or ever existed at all, is a matter that can be proved conclusively only by the discovery of either a live specimen or of fresh bones in association with the remains of men. But if they do exist, the question that immediately springs to mind is, could they be dinosaurs? The answer, perhaps rather surprisingly, is yes.

The name dinosaur, which means simply "terrible lizard," is a popular, not a scientific term. It would be best reserved for two groups of reptiles that are thought to be totally extinct, but it is also customarily given to the larger extinct members of all the other groups including ancestors of the tortoises, crocodiles and lizards. Neither in its general nor its restricted sense, however, does the name dinosaur necessarily imply primitiveness of structure, great geological age or even large size, for there are many medium, small and tiny ones. The crocodiles as a group are just as old and individually much larger than many dinosaurs, while the tortoises belong to one of the most primitive of all reptilian stocks. The little lizard-shaped tuatara which still lives on the islands off New Zealand, is, in the general sense, a dinosaur and it is much more primitive and comes from an older stock than those two groups which we call dinosaurs in the more restricted sense.

This puts the whole matter in an entirely different light. If the tortoises, the tuatara and the crocodiles have managed to survive from the age of reptiles, there is really no reason why members of the other groups, some much less primitive and including those that we may choose to call dinosaurs, should not also have survived. The majority of the reptiles disappeared at the end of what is called the Cretaceous period, after which the more active and clever mammals took over. But there is no reason why some might not have lingered on until today in the vast and isolated swamps of Africa—the one part of the world that has remained tropical and comparatively stable since the Cretaceous period and which was almost entirely unaffected by the great ice ages and the mountain-building disturbances of intervening times.

It is indeed a very curious business that merits our consideration and, in my opinion, some active investigation. Can the whole thing be the product of wishful thinking? Can all these big-game hunters, animal collectors, game wardens, and princely African writers of official minutes be pure sensation seekers or under the influence? Did Professor Koldewey just go daft and throw away his high scientific standing with carefree abandon?

There could be dinosaurs alive today, so let us try to maintain what should be the true scientific spirit and simply say that, as yet, there is no positive evidence that they do still exist.

## A Live Pterodactyl?

*From* The Illustrated London News *for February 9, 1856, p. 166*

"Very like a whale"—"A discovery of great scientific importance has just been made at Culmont (Haute Marne). Some men employed in cutting a tunnel which is to unite the St. Dizier and Nancy railways, had just thrown down an enormous block of stone by means of gunpowder, and were in the act of breaking it to pieces, when from a cavity in it they suddenly saw emerge a living being of monstrous form. This creature, which belongs to the class of animals hitherto considered to be extinct, has a very long neck, and a mouth filled with sharp teeth. It stands on four long legs, which are united together by two membranes, doubtless intended to support the animal in the air, and are armed with four claws terminated by long and crooked talons. Its general form resembles that of a bat, differing only in its size, which is that of a large goose. Its membranous wings, when spread out, measure from tip to tip 3 meters, 22 centimeters (nearly 10 feet, 17 inches). Its colour is a livid black; its skin is naked, thick, and oily; its intestines only contained a colourless liquid like clear water. On reaching the light this monster gave some signs of life, by shaking its wings, but soon after expired, uttering a hoarse cry. This strange creature, to which may be given the name of living fossil, has been brought to Gray, where a naturalist, well versed in the study of paleontology, immediately recognised it as belonging to the genus *Pterodactylus anas*, many fossil remains of which have been found among the strata which geologists have designated by the name of lias. The rock in which this monster was discovered belongs precisely to that formation the deposit of which is so old that goelogists date it more than a million years back. The cavity in which the animal was lodged forms an exact hollow mould of its body, which indicates that it was completely enveloped with the sedimentary deposit. *Presse Graylouse.*"

# A Monster from the Trinity Alps

*From the* San Francisco Examiner *for January 18, 1960*

In January 1960 an interesting story popped up in a few northern California newspapers. Vern Harden, an animal handler, told the story of how he had been fishing in a remote Trinity Alps lake with piano wire and a shark hook, and had caught an enormous salamander—eight feet, four inches long!

The Trinity Alps and a large section of northern California is very rough and unknown country. In spite of some roads built in relatively recent times, there may actually be pockets of land essentially unexplored. It is the same area from which comes so many Bigfoot reports.

Giant salamanders are known of course in Japan and China on about the same latitude and altitude and the same general type of habitat. These Asian salamanders grow to six feet long at maximum. The largest known salamander in the U.S. is the Mississippi Delta "Hellbender," about two feet long, and one from California called the "giant salamander," although it is only a foot long.

Harden's story was told to Victor Twitty, a biologist at Stanford, who was quoted as saying "spectacular, if true." Dr. Robert C. Stebbins, a zoologist at the University of California heard the story and was skeptical but interested. He is a well-known expert on reptiles and remembers a story told by Stanford biologist George Myers. Myers found an old fisherman who fished in the Sacramento River. This fisherman had a salamander three and a half feet long in his bathtub. He was unable to get it from the fisherman or learn exactly where it was caught but described it as resembling the Japanese salamander. This is rather suggestive—after all this creature seen by Myers is close to twice the size of the largest known salamander in the U.S. Perhaps it was a small specimen of the giant species.

But what happened to the eight foot beast? Harden said a blizzard came on and he had to abandon the reptile. So he brought out no proof. One could consider this a suspicious tale of the "big fish that got away" variety. Indeed, a priest, Father Bernard Hubbard of Santa Clara College, made quite derogatory statements about Harden's report. News stories are not explicit of course, but one suspects some rancor between the two people accounts for the questioning of Harden's story. For Father Hubbard has a brother, Capt. John Hubbard, a retired mining engineer and one who has collected about all that has been collected concerning the giant salamanders of Northern California. Over a period of 50 years, fishermen in the area have reported seeing such creatures, some of them nine feet long! The Hubbards seem to accept these other stories on the salamanders while rejecting Harden's.

And it seems the talk at the time of fitting up an expedition to look for the creatures wasn't just talk. In the fall of 1960, Professor Stebbins, Dr. Rogers of Chico State College, and Dr. Cohen of Modesto Junior College went into the area with a group of explorer scouts to look for the giants. Stebbins stated that he hoped to find some giant salamanders but wouldn't be too surprised if he didn't. So the expedition planned on investigating the other reptile life in the area—whatever its size.

Unfortunately we have no report on that 1960 expedition and its findings. We suspect they were negative since all the news stories on the animal come only from a local level. Yet there is strong reason to think that some giant species of this reptile live in the area. If scientists can't find this creature whose existence wouldn't greatly upset scientific circles, it's probably not too surprising that they can't find the Bigfoot in the same area, whose existence would upset the applecart of many an anthropologist.

*Sources*
"Father Hubbard Spotlights Salamanders." *Humboldt Times,* Jan. 24, 1960
"Professors trying to unravel old legend of Lizard." *Humboldt Times,* Sept. 1, 1960
"Sea Monster in Trinity Alps Lake?" *San Francisco Examiner,* Jan. 18, 1960

## Dinosaurs on the Loose Again

*From* Strange Creatures from Time and Space, *by John Keel (New York, Fawcett Books)*

In the summer of 1969 I received a couple of letters passing along rumors that a dinosaur was roaming about Texas. According to one story, said saurian had hauled a car 200 feet off the road and killed its driver. Attempts to track these tales down proved futile, so the Texas dinosaur was entered into our "hearsay" file and forgotten.

But from the London *Sunday Express,* of July 26, 1970:

Troops and police are hunting a multi-legged monster which is reported to be roaming woods near Forli in Central Italy. The monster—some call it a dinosaur—was first seen last Tuesday by Antonio Samorani, a 48-year-old peasant. He reported that he had been chased by a "huge scaly thing at least 15 feet long. It walked on thick legs and its breath was searing hot. I ran for my life and it followed me for a couple of hundred yards."

Police were sceptical at first but changed their minds when they saw large footprints in a glade near where Samorani says he saw the monster. Police Chief Dr. Pedoni said: "We are convinced some sort of creature of colossal size is hiding in the woods. Three other people have seen it. We are combing the area with armed police and soldiers with nets. If possible we want to catch it alive. Over a thousand guns will be out looking for this animal when the hunting season opens on August 1. If the local hunters reach it first we will be powerless to stop them."

# PART FOUR
## FORTEAN PHENOMENA

# OF PHANTOMS AND MEN

*It has been said of ghost stories that they are "the best docu-
mented" occurrences in human history. Unfortunately for the
splendid ideal of documentation, we can accept this statement only
with a grain of salt. But since an authentic Fortean attitude
combines the highest degree of skepticism with the most serious
attempt to be completely open to strange facts, the psychic domain
is the one that poses perhaps the largest number of problems.*

*The will to believe and simultaneously not to believe is very
strong, and the will to deceive is equally strong. We do not take a
stand on "credibility," since it is doubtful that there exists a useful
position to take. The presence of phantoms in one's house is
perhaps irrational—the word itself may be somewhat strange—but
has what passes for "rational" ever been anything more than a
belief in a particular group of histories of phantoms?*

125

# Poltergeists in New Zealand

*From* The Evening Post *of Wellington, New Zealand, March 25, 26, and 27, 1963*

"While 12 policemen and more than 20 civilians searched the area, the Ohiro Lodge guest house at Brooklyn (a suburb of Wellington, N.Z.) was bombarded with stones, apparently from a catapult, for seven-and-a-half hours last night and early this morning." So began *The Evening Post* of Wellington on March 25, 1963, little suspecting it was beginning a classical and interesting story of that mysterious and somewhat disquieting fellow, the poltergeist.

"The owners of the house and 15 lodgers had a sleepless night as they helped the Police search in vain and then were disturbed time and again when they did ultimately try to get to bed."

Stones crashed into the house and smashed almost every window. Occasionally, policemen and inhabitants of the boarding house were hit, but no serious harm occurred. The stones were many but every one hit this house precisely—no other house in the area reported any hits. On the first night 30 stones and 4 *pennies* struck the house. [Those not acquainted with New Zealand pennies should note it is a large copper coin and not to be trifled with. It must weigh almost as much as a U.S. half dollar.] The barrage began with a penny smashing a window on the north end of the veranda at 9:30 P.M. The boarders of the house huddled in the kitchen in back of the house as the stones and pennies smashed down.

The police showed up in force and were mystified. Obviously no one could hurl the missiles at the house with the force observed and stay out of sight. The idea that some machine must be involved was suggested. But nothing was found anywhere. The proprietors of the guest house, Mr. and Mrs. R.A. Beatty, said "I can't imagine who did it, or why." They noted that some macrocarpo trees, more than 100 years old, had been pulled out recently on the property but didn't think this had anything to do with the attack.

The next night the attack, much to everyone's dismay, continued. It began at 7:30 P.M. and went on until after 1:00 A.M. Everyone in the house was aggravated at the loss of a second night's sleep. The lodgers were talking about leaving.

The police showed up again, and with the lodgers and a police dog, searched everywhere and found—nothing. A police radar set was brought in and set up—but the stone throwing stopped just as it was ready! Again, nobody could figure out why anyone would be doing this to the house and its occupants.

Finally someone suggested that it might be a poltergeist. It was also discovered that there was a precedent in Wellington for such activities. Forty years ago a house on Mount Victoria experienced a similar attack—a prolonged bombardment of stones. A mother and her son lived in the house and despite intensive searching, nothing was found to explain the attack.

The next night (the third) 600 people turned up for the show. Anonymous threats were received on the phone that someone would be killed. At 6:30 P.M. the performance began with the arrival of the first penny. The crowd cheered as each penny or stone struck the house. Some of the stones turned out to be pumice on inspection. There is no pumice in Wellington, but pumice exists in certain volcanic parts of New Zealand. Sometimes pumice is washed up on the beach in Wellington. The largest stone of the bombardment arrived at 8 P.M., and was over 3 inches in diameter. The barrage stopped at 9:30 P.M.

The crowd outside the house helped the show along the third night by throwing stones and pennies themselves. The police tried to catch these people, but the crowd was so thick it was impossible. They no doubt scented the possibility of pinning the whole thing on one of these fellows but they were sadly disappointed.

There was never any noise associated with the arrival of any stone. The police could not explain how any mechanical device could store up so much energy and suddenly release it without some noise. The stones just suddenly appeared and struck the house.

Someone suggested that "a metallurgist" be employed to determine the location from which the missiles were coming. In this case, it might have been a bit more sensible to suggest calling in the local priest.* Or at least the weatherman.

After 9:30 P.M. on the third night, the phenomena stopped entirely. The house was afterwards demolished and a block of flats put up in Oct. 1969, but no unusual events of any kind have been reported either during the demolition or in the new apartments.

*And here's a clutch of ghosts, beasties, and things walking in the night. Every story is authentic. Every story could be multiplied by a hundred: you need only read my report "The Mysterious Present" in the magazine* Nostradamus. *Don't ask me for any explanations, because I don't have any.*

## Family Flees from Ghost House

*From the* Sunday Morning Herald *of Sydney, Australia, for February 25, 1970*

A young couple and their four-months-old daughter have left their home in a Newcastle suburb because they think it is haunted. Mr. Michael Cooke, 19, and his wife, Dianne, 18, spent their last night on Sunday in the half-house they rent as a flat in Hereford St., Stockton. They moved into a neighbor's house on Monday and Mr. Cooke spent today unsuccessfully looking for another home.

The couple are firmly convinced the house is haunted by the ghost of a man. They refuse to go inside unless accompanied by police or friends. To even a casual observer their fear is real, and infectious.

They named eight friends and neighbors who had heard or seen mysterious happenings in the spacious white weatherboard house in the past two weeks. "Last night I saw a horrible white face looking out of one of the windows as I walked past," Mr. Cooke said. "The eyes were white with green in the middle. I was so scared the tears just ran out of my eyes. That was the end. I was thinking of buying

---

*The sensibleness of this escapes me—Paul J. Willis.

the house, but I'll never live there again."

Last night, Constable W. Manning, of Stockton, searched and locked the house after 10:00 P.M. This morning, the beds were disturbed, but the windows were still locked from the inside. Constable Manning and Mr. Cooke searched the house and ceiling today without finding any trace of a human intruder. Constable Manning had no comment to offer, but the incident was recorded at Stockton police station with typical official caution as "alleged haunted house in Hereford St., Stockton."

The other half of the house is occupied by the owner, a 67-year-old woman who has been a patient in a Newcastle hospital for a week. Mrs. Cooke said the owner asked her to look after her flat while she was away. "I made the beds four times this week, and each morning they were rumpled," she said. "We thought at first it was a burglar, but when things began happening without reason we got scared."

Mr. and Mrs. Cooke described how a doorknob shook loudly even though the wire door on the outside was securely bolted. "My baby is only four months old and can't sit up by herself, but late at night we have seen her sit up as if something is pulling her upright by the arms," Mrs. Cooke said. "Then the baby screams and falls back onto the cot. Sometimes the baby's toys are found moved from place to place. We have been here a month. The previous tenant told me he was awakened one night by something he could not see shaking his shoulder. The bloke here before him woke up to find someone peering at him."

Jenny Zrodlowski, 17, a neighbor, said today she saw a figure standing behind a glass partition between the two flats yesterday afternoon, but when she and Mrs. Cooke investigated they could find no one.

## A Recent Canadian Poltergeist

*From* The Edmonton Journal, *Edmonton, Canada, for February 16, 1970*

St. Catharines, Ont. (CP)—There seems to be a weight-lifting, furniture-moving spirit hanging around a St. Catharines family's apartment these days. Two doctors, two lawyers, two priests, and a group of St. Catharines policemen say they have witnessed the spirit in action.

They say a chair, with an 11-year-old boy in it, floated seven inches off the ground, but a policeman who then tried to lift it couldn't. Beds have tilted on end and bureaus have moved from wall to wall.

A veteran of 23 years on the city police force said Saturday: "I know of at least five officers who have witnessed these happenings who . . . are convinced that something supernatural is taking place."

Police, who prefer to keep the family's name private, say they are bringing in physicists and other experts to investigate. Utilities company officials, fire inspectors, and the city building inspector all have failed to come up with a logical explanation.

The family has lived in the apartment for more than 10 years but the trouble with the furniture began only in the last couple of weeks.

## Walchuks Move, Ghost Doesn't

*From* The Evening Review *for March 14, 1970*

A St. Catharines family whose 11-year-old son was the target for supernatural events solved the problem by moving from their apartment. A St. Catharines policeman, one of the persons who witnessed furniture moving for no visible reason in the apartment, said Peter Walchuk and his family have moved from their Church St. home.

In late January, the lad became a catalyst for strange furniture movements. Beds balanced on three legs, pictures flew from the wall and a chair the boy was sitting in overturned. City police officers, doctors, and priests say they witnessed the events.

Now the boy has moved, the furniture causes no problems. There is no indication the unexplainable movements, said by some to be caused by a poltergeist (a mischievous ghost that plays tricks mainly on children), followed the boy to his new home.

During the activity in this case, John Gibson, a *Hamilton Spectator* reporter was told by the police to get out of town fast or go to jail. The police said they didn't like the way the press was covering the story. Gibson pointed out that Canada enjoyed freedom of the press and covered the story. Hats off, Mr. Gibson!

## "Spirit" Holds Home in Grip of Terror

*From* The Edmonton Journal, *Edmonton, Canada, for November 11, 1969*

Gillingham, England (AP)—A quiet seaside home has become a residence of fear, where a three-year-old girl contorts in apparent rage at the sight of a crucifix. The baby has been taken over by a malignant spirit, says her mother, Christine Adams. A supernatural presence has possessed the girl and the modest, terraced house in the Kent coast town.

The terror began a year ago, said Mrs. Adams, when lights flickered on and off, furniture moved, closed doors opened, ashtrays tumbled off tables, and warm rooms suddenly became icily cold. "Most frightening of all, though, was the transformation of Carol," she said. The child began holding conversations with another person, using words no child of her age could know, sometimes answering herself in another adult voice.

"Sometimes we could hear somebody singing—it sounded like a lullaby—while she was talking at the same time," the mother said. She and her husband placed a wooden cross in their living room in an attempt to combat the presence.

"When Carol went near the cross her face contorted," Mrs. Adams, 27, recalled. "She would bunch up her fingers into claws and bare her teeth. It was frightening."

Neighbor Marjorie English told of the day she saw Carol hanging out an upstairs window. "I rushed next door to tell her mother, but she told me it was impossible—the windows were locked and nailed down. When Mr. Adams got home, he checked, and the windows could not be opened." She added, "I have always laughed at this sort of thing. But I have seen too much."

Mrs. English's son Graham, 17, said he and Mrs. Adams heard noises from Carol's room one night and they both went upstairs to investigate. The child was "stuffed right inside a pillow case."

"We got her out and carried her downstairs, but when we went back a few minutes later, we found the cot had been remade and the pillowcase, which had been thrown aside, was back on the pillow."

Said Mrs. Adams: "I am convinced a supernatural presence has taken over the house and is appearing through Carol." She summoned a medium, Elizabeth Langridge, to help.

"We did not see anything but we did sense undesirable influences," she said. "A spirit entity was using this child."

## Torres Strait's Island of Fear

*From the* Sunday Mirror *of Sydney, Australia, August 30, 1970*

Fear is keeping people off a tropical paradise island in the Torres Strait. The haunted island, Gabba, 70 miles north of Cape York, is covered in rain forests and wild flowers. Its trees are laden with tropical fruits, its streams flow with crystal-clear water, and it has magnificent beaches. Its bays and inlets team with crabs, lobsters, prawns, and game fish. The August temperature is a perfect 85 to 90 degrees, and it will stay that way most of the year.

But Torres Strait islanders shun this Garden of Eden like the plague. They are quite sure that to stay on Gabba after sunset means death.

Jimmy Levi, a native from Thursday Island, told about Gabba and the "Witch" which haunts it. He is engineer of the ply boat *Melbidir* and is said to know the cluster of Torres Strait islands better than anyone else.

"She is like the devil," he said in the shy, quiet manner typical of the islanders. "We have been told by our fathers, she will kill anyone who stays there at night. She will hurl huge rocks down on them and crush them."

Jimmy said Gabba was once one of the most heavily-populated islands in Torres Strait. But according to the legend, about 300 years ago a terrible disease spread across Gabba after some of the islanders ate poisonous turtles. The survivors took to their canoes and paddled to another island. All except one old woman, who, wailing and screaming at the people in the canoes, dragged herself up into the rocks.

After that, anyone who went to Gabba heard weird wailings, noises, and horrible screams. As soon as darkness fell, huge boulders crashed down on them. Only a few escaped to tell the tale. Shaking with fear, they had told how they had seen the terrifying figure of an old woman on the island's gigantic balancing rock, screaming and laughing.

"Everyone believes it—even the young people," Jimmy said. They lower their voices when they talk about the witch. "It is very bad because Gabba is such a good island. It has some of the best fish in the islands. But the Rock Witch will not let anyone live there."

## Vampire in a Miniskirt Scares Police

*From the* London Mirror *for November 9, 1967*

A mini-skirted "vampire" who stalks a holiday beach was being hunted by police last night. The police were told that the vampire had been terrorizing people at night on a beach near the Brazilian city of Manaus. Several people who were attacked described the vampire as "a blonde woman with sharp and pointed teeth, wearing a mini-skirt and black stockings." Two small round marks were said to have been found near the jugular vein of a child who was bitten. One report from Manaus added that, out of thirty policemen detailed to probe the vampire mystery, seventeen had cried off.

## Vampire Hunt by Mr. Blood

*From the* London Mirror *for March 15, 1970*

The "undead satan-like creature" that legend says lurks in the cemetery where Karl Marx is buried eluded 100 vampire hunters yesterday. The hunt brought vampire expert Alan Blood to London's Highgate cemetery . . . and several spine-chilling frights to the hunters. Crowds gathered in the darkness before dawn after watching a television interview on Friday night in which a man said he was going to exorcise an evil spirit he claimed he had seen three times. Mr. Anthony Robinson, 27, of Ostel Road, Hampstead, went to the cemetery after hearing of the torchlight hunt. He said: "I heard a high-pitched noise. Then I saw something grey moving slowly across the road. It terrified me." The vampire expert, history teacher Alan Blood, 25, traveled from Chelmsford, Essex, after he saw 24-year-old David Farrant on BBC television talk of his plans to stake the vampire through the heart with a wooden cross. Mr. Blood said, "This whole thing was timed wrongly—there were too many people around, which would disturb any undead spirit in the cemetery."

## Full Moon Shines...
## A Man Hunts for a Vampire

*From the* London Mirror, *undated*

Carrying a wooden cross and a stake, 24-year-old Alan [sic] Farrant sneaked into a graveyard at midnight to hunt down a vampire. With the aid of a torch and the light of a full moon, he searched among the tombs. Then the silence was broken by the sound of a car. . . . It was a police car. Farrant's expedition was called off. And instead, he had to explain exactly what he thought he was doing in London's Highgate cemetery at that time of night. "I have been told that a vampire rises from the catacombs at the cemetery. Had the police not arrived, I would have entered the

catacombs and inspected the coffins. Upon finding this supernatural being, I would have driven my stake through it's heart and
then run away." The magistrate said Farrant should see a doctor,
and remanded him to custody.

# Man Dies in an Ambush
# Set to Trap a Vampire

*From the* London Mirror *of February 27, 1969*

Villagers were certain that a "vampire" was spiriting away some
of them at night. So the villagers—in Korogwe, East Africa—
decided to lay an ambush. And because they thought the "vampire"
was a European, they killed the first white man to drive into the
ambush—German plantation manager Klaus Kaufmann, 41. He
was beaten and hacked to death with long knives and spears after a
duck hunting trip. Yesterday, one of the seven men accused of
murdering Kaufmann told a court in Dar-es-Salaam that villagers
became frightened about the "vampire" after several people had
mysteriously vanished.

# Vampire Moths

*From the* Edmonton Journal, *Edmonton, Canada, for December 13,*
*1968*

Dr. Hans Banziger, a Swiss entomologist working in Malaya has
observed the noxious habits of a skin-piercing, blood-sucking moth.
The nocturnal vampire called "calyptra-eustrigata" could be a living
example of evolution in progress. Some of these moths have
developed mouth parts strong enough to penetrate the tough skin of
mammals. Dr. Banziger has seen the moth suck blood from buffalo,
deer, tapir, and antelopes. Human guinea pigs say "it felt like being
stabbed with a hot needle."

# A Vampire Frightens the People
# of Humahuaca, Argentina

*From an unnamed Mexico City newspaper for January 7, 1969*

Jujuy, Argentina, Jan. 6, 1969 (UPI)—A gigantic vampire which weighs between 5 and 6 kilograms according to witnesses, has terrorized the population of the gorge of Humahuaca, a picturesque geographic zone in this province of northeast Argentina.

The muledriver Meliton Juarez, one of the witnesses, affirmed he was attacked by the enormous creature while riding on his mule. His mount was frightened when the vampire made several passes over them. Juarez added that the vampire has a "horrible" aspect and he was able to use his whip several times to chase it away. He said he thought the strange bat intended to land on the mule and suck its blood.

The neighbors from the gorge presumed that this was the same vampire that recently made many incursions on the ranches of the area where it appeared that numerous domestic fowls died, having had their blood sucked.

Zoological experts say that the apparition of vampires of such menacing size is supported by an episode which occurred at a place in Mexico several years ago, when two monstrous vampires killed a woman and man while they slept.

# THE STONING OF THE HOSPITAL OF ARCACHON

## Jacques Bergier

*It is the social position of the principal witness that gives value and originality to the strange story I am about to tell. Doctor A. Cuénot is a member of a famous family of biologists. He has a scientific, but also an open, mind.*

*Dr. Cuénot has written a book,* Les Certitudes irrationnelles *(Editions Planète), which is a model of both intellectual rigor and broad-mindedness. In his preface, Aimé Michel very correctly states: "There exists as yet no science of the complete human being. We do not even know if there exists a complete human being. Of all the possible hypotheses concerning our future, the least insane and the most improbable is that this future is boundless and that we have scarcely begun the exploration of our own selves. The extraordinary successes of the human genius that we are presently witnessing reflect back to us the image of a child who has just discovered a new toy."*

*The following story shows that the powers of the complete human being are still largely unknown to us.*

137

*The place:* An orthopedic hospital in the French Atlantic coastal city of Arcachon, a few miles southwest of Bordeaux. For twenty-five years, the hospital had been under the direction of Dr. Cuénot. It specialized in the treatment of tuberculosis of the bone.

*The time:* May–September, 1963.

*The phenomenon:* A bombardment of the hospital with pebbles, stones, fragments of brick, and objects of undetermined origin.

More than 300 of these objects fell at all hours of the day and at nightfall. The patients stretched out in their chairs seemed to be the particular targets. The phenomenon was linked to the presence of a seventeen-year-old girl whom we shall call Jacqueline, and who was herself heavily stoned.

From the psychological and social points of view, it should be mentioned that the phenomenon was preceded by the announcement on April 19, 1963, of the sale of the hospital, which was to close on September 30. It was this announcement which seems to have set off reactions on the part of . . . an unknown party.

To speak about the "collective unconscious" of the patients at the hospital is equivalent to speaking of the soporific power of opium. These are words, nothing more.

The stone throwing was aimed first at a young woman whom we shall call Angelina. After her departure from the hospital and the arrival of Jacqueline on June 16, the phenomenon became more pronounced. The information given by Doctor Cuénot in his book, mentioned above, and in certain publications, in particular the *Revue métapsychique*, make an analysis possible.

In most cases, the stones fell vertically; oblique paths were rare. They fell through the foliage of three plane trees on the hospital grounds, at a speed that was very low in comparison with the speed they should have had when falling from this height.

The maximum number of throws per day was 48. The local police, to whom a complaint was made on August 28, seem to have regarded Doctor Cuénot as insane, which is in strong contrast to the open-minded attitude of the German police in the Rosenheim matter (discussed later in this book). On the other hand, the Metapsychic Institute sent Professor Tocquet to investigate the matter, and his contribution is very interesting.

No hoax seems to have been found. When questioned, Jacqueline denied that she had any role in the matter. The general opinion at the hospital was that a group of practical jokers was involved, but it was never learned who they were or how they got into and left the hospital.

The stone throwing stopped on September 1, 1963, but was followed by other phenomena, notably the striking of blows in or against doors that began to open spontaneously. On September 4, bolts were installed, and then everything stopped.

Obviously there is no definitive explanation. In the best of good faith, Doctor Cuénot brought up the rational hypothesis of a madman armed with a catapult and firing from a distance. But such a madman was never found, and no other building in Arcachon was stoned. Personally, I do not believe this hypothesis at all. Nor do I believe in the idea of a joke played by patients. The patients were at the point where they watched themselves, and a practical joke would have been discovered.

Thus we are obliged to consider the paranormal hypothesis, which repels us because of its fantastic aspect. The various pebbles, stones, and bricks do not appear to have come from the hospital buildings (although these were decaying), but from another source.

Supposing that this source—let us say a construction site—were about a half-mile away. This conjures up the idea of fragments of brick rising into the air, floating through it at a relatively slow speed, then reaching the hospital, all of which requires considerable work against gravitation. It is difficult to conceive that the nervous system of one or several patients could have supplied this energy without catastrophe resulting for the patient.

If a paranormal phenomenon was involved, it utilized an energy that is present in nature but about which we know nothing at present.

In one case, during August, a patient who was a Paris policeman, hence theoretically a qualified witness and a good observer, saw one of the stones begin to fall from a room on the second floor of an unused building of the hospital. There immediately followed a mad dash to this room. It was empty, and its door was locked.

In another strange incident, one of the patients, who had been liberally pelted, began to scream, "That's enough! Isn't this idiot ever going to stop?!" The phenomenon ceased. It began a half hour later, but more timidly—as if the phenomenon in question were capable of reacting. . . .

Phenomena of this type are too frequent to permit attribution of all of them to practical jokers or insane people. To be sure, in one case in Bordeaux the police arrested an insane young man who was pelting an entire neighborhood with a stone thrower. There are also numerous cases of insane snipers, some of whom were arrested. But in a great majority of cases, falls of stones and sometimes chunks of ice have no accepted explanation at the present time.

Needless to say, there is no question of collective or other hallucinations, since the stones remain after the phenomena.

Doctor Cuénot made a psychological analysis of Jacqueline, which, although very interesting, revealed nothing particularly abnormal. The girl did not appear frightened, and she even found it quite funny to be the center of a phenomenon that no adult could explain. She had no scores to settle with anyone, and basically there was nothing to prove that she had any relationship, paranormal or otherwise, with the phenomenon. The hospital itself was quite old and dilapidated, but there were no paranormal or supernatural legends in its history.

What does this mean?

This means that, as in the Rosenheim case, we are in the presence of a power unknown to science, a power that appears to differ from scientific phenomena in one essential aspect: the manifestation of consciousness. This power attaches itself to one particular being—in the case of the hospital, first Angelina and then Jacqueline. It appears to be sensitive to human reactions, and no longer appears once the human subject departs.

Then it attaches itself to another subject. An animal, a bird for example, may behave in this way. The problem is that we know no case of behavior of this type among birds. Birds (magpies, for example) have been known to steal bright objects, but we know of no birds that persecute people. Moreover, a bird would have been seen.

Is it possible that we are surrounded by invisible animals— "condemned things," as Ambrose Bierce said?

This hypothesis is disturbing, but there is not the slightest proof of it. In Carcassonne in 1969, a victim of a fall of stones equipped himself with a bag of flour and a camera. When the stones began to fall, he threw his bag of flour into the air and then took a photograph (published in the newspaper *France-Soir*), which shows a kind of shape. The picture is not very convincing. It can be accepted that it resulted from the action of the flour sticking to an invisible object. It can also be accepted that it is a hoax. I would require many more proofs before I would believe in the existence of a new, invisible animal kingdom.

Nor do I believe in the spiritualistic explanations—phantoms, ectoplasms, etc.—because, in the laboratory, this type of manifestation has always and without exception proved to be a hoax. (In this connection, see my notes in Robert Amadou's *Les Grands Mediums* in the series La Tour Saint-Jacques, published by Editions Denöel.)

Solely for the sake of humor, I shall mention the hypothesis of Professor Nandor Fodor. According to this Hungarian psychoanalyst and worthy disciple of Freud, the stone-throwing spirits may be phantoms not of persons but of complexes! In other words, there may exist persons so twisted that after their deaths their complexes remain as knots in space-time.

Let us return to more serious possibilities. The American physicist George O. Smith, inventor of the short-distance rocket and a science-fiction author, has advanced the hypothesis that rapping spirits are produced by natural forces that are usually completely neutralized in space.

According to Smith, the electrical currents in the brain may break this equilibrium and produce whirling movements that we will one day learn to guide, but for the moment, they are controlled solely by unconscious impulses.

This may seem sufficiently plausible to justify further research.

It must be hoped that this research will give us the key to the puzzle of rapping and stone-throwing spirits and, perhaps, of antigravitation.

# THE ELECTRIC PHENOMENON
# OF ROSENHEIM
## Jacques Bergier

*The extraordinary phenomena that manifested themselves in November, 1967, at Rosenheim in Bavaria, Germany, have been investigated by psychologists and parapsychologists, and by Professor Hans Bender, Director of the Institute for the Frontiers of Psychology in Freiburg-im-Breisgau. Two physicists, F. Karger and G. Zicha, have also made a study of the phenomena.*

*Since the days of the Romans, if not earlier, parapsychological, psychokinetic phenomena have been recognized by the fact that there is an absorption of energy: the temperature drops. But the Rosenheim phenomenon also absorbs electrical energy, a completely new event that deserves serious study.*

In November, 1967, the eight-foot-long luminescent tubes in the ceiling of an attorney's office in Rosenheim began to become unscrewed of their own power. Switches tripped for no reason. Liquids from the photocopying machines came out of their containers and made everything wet. The four telephones rang simultaneously; there was no one at the other end. The telephone bills were enormous; the number for the correct time had been called thousands of times.

A preliminary study of the phenomenon was made by the electric company and by the Siemens Company, as well as the German television networks, which presented the phenomenon in two episodes.

Then Professor Bender was called in. He found that the phenomenon always occurred in the presence of a nineteen-year-old employee whom he called Anne-Marie Sch.

Upon the complaint of the head of the office, Mr. Adam, the criminal police began their own investigation, the outcome of which was that no hoax could be detected. It was noted, for example, that a picture hung on the wall had rotated 320 degrees, and that this rotation seems to have been due to paranormal forces.

The luminescent tubes were replaced by incandescent bulbs. These proceeded to burst.

In the presence of the experts, drawers opened by themselves, and a file cabinet weighing 385 pounds moved one foot away from the wall.

Miss Sch. became ill and returned home, where the same phenomenon occurred. She changed jobs; identical events took place in her new office. Measuring instruments showed that the phenomenon absorbed electrical power. The same phenomenon called the correct time number five times a minute, without touching the dial!

The impulses appeared directly in the line. Several measurements made on Miss Sch. showed that the phenomenon was linked to states of hypertension. Insofar as could be judged, she had no evil or hostile intention; her entire attitude seemed indicative rather of a desire to help her employer, Mr. Adam, who was greatly disturbed by this phenomenon. Despite the fact that she was on a medical leave of absence, Miss Sch. came to the office every time she was requested to do so, and this made it possible to establish a definite correlation between the phenomenon and her presence. She also submitted to parapsychological tests. During her periods of tension, she showed faculties of clairvoyance that were on a high level.

The most recent news of this girl is very sad. The phenomenon in question apparently followed her along the street and into a bowling alley managed by her fiancé. The entire electrical recording apparatus of the bowling alley went out of order, and the fiancé, terrified, broke the engagement, whereupon Miss Sch. became ill. This drama shows, in any case, that she had no intention of arranging these manifestations, even if she had had the power.

The manifestations in question, and particularly the calls to the automatic telephone number for the correct time, require an extremely high mental power and the exercise of senses that we human beings do not have or that are not known to us. What is involved here is the long-distance emission of electrical signals and their transmission along a line with the precision of about a millisecond. No human being normally possesses such powers, and this is the disturbing aspect of this phenomenon.

The study made by the physicists F. Karger and G. Zicha shows that the Rosenheim phenomenon seemed to be able to cause the needle of a measuring instrument to move, without the presence of any natural phenomenon to explain it. The following natural causes have been examined and eliminated:

1. Variations of voltage in the lines (despite the deflection of the recorder, the voltage remained constant);
2. High-frequency demodulated voltage combining with a nonlinear distinctive wavelength (no signal to the tension probe, test made with a generator having a 100-watt signal);
3. An electrostatic charge;
4. Static outside magnetic field (no signal to the magnetic field probe);
5. Poor contact in the electronic amplification system; me-

chanism out of order in the recording device (the same phenomena occurred with a second, brand new recording device, and so this hypothesis must be rejected);

6.    Effects of ultrasounds or infrasounds; strong vibrations;

7.    The hypothesis of fraud by human intervention in the recording operation was completely eliminated.

When a microphone was planted, a signal with an amplitude of ten volts was detected. This seems to have been the result of a paranormal mechanical pressure on the crystal of the microphone. No sound was heard. The microphone was under surveillance, and no one had gone near it.

When the abnormal impulses of the current were recorded, movements of the recording pencil corresponding to currents of fifty amperes were found. No current was detected.

The recorders used were all standard models in perfect adjustment. The rotation of a picture was recorded on a cassette by an Ampex Video Recorder device of the type commonly used in television—the first time that a device of this type recorded ghosts.

A case is known in Great Britain in which a television camera being used in an attempt to film a ghost in a haunted house was pushed by invisible hands and fell into a stairwell, just missing a cameraman. But to date, no one had ever seen standard electronic equipment record phenomena of paranormal origin. For this reason, the Rosenheim case is historic. As regards the electronic aspect, it should be added that the phenomenon continued when the premises were supplied by batteries without being connected into the local supply circuit. This eliminates once and for all the possibility of irregularities in the supply circuit, which, moreover, would have been detected by the maintenance service who maintained a Siemens Unireg recorder on the current feed line throughout the period of these events. The only interesting thing to be found in the report of the maintenance service is the testimony of an employee, who noted that when Miss Sch. passed through the corridor the light bulbs swayed behind her.

A medical examination of Miss Sch. showed disturbing muscular spasms of a hysterical type, which ceased when she left the attorney's office.

Miss Sch.'s parents were opposed to questioning and treatment by hypnosis. Perhaps they were right, since hypnotism is a phenomenon about which little is known even today.

To summarize: statements of witnesses, police reports, reports by the electric power maintenance service in Rosenheim, and reports by parapsychologists and physicians all agree on one fact—phenomena of an unknown nature occurred at Rosenheim.

These phenomena are of the "poltergeist" (or "rapping spirits") type, which are found everywhere and in every period. They are frequently accompanied by the presence of adolescents or girls, but this is not always the case. The English writer Arthur Machen, who carried out several investigations of this subject for newspapers, received a great deal of verified evidence of cases in which no adolescent was present. This evidence included a genuine persecution in a London family boardinghouse that took only adult boarders of fairly advanced age and a statement by an Anglican bishop who had seen a hut in Africa literally shredded and reduced to bits in the presence of several hundred witnesses. This hut, which had been evacuated, was inhabited by an elderly couple, and no adolescent was present.

Thus we have no hypothesis or even any correlation sufficiently precise to link the phenomenon with known natural forces.

At Rosenheim, we find for the first time a correlation with electricity. It is possible that the same correlation could have been found if instruments for detecting and recording electrical phenomena had been available in the past.

Pliny the Elder describes a case very similar to that of Rosenheim. Obviously, however, he had neither the ideas nor the instruments that would have permitted him to determine whether electrical phenomena were occurring.

The importance of Doctors Karger and Zicha, who studied the phenomenon on the scientific level, must be emphasized. They are members of the Max Planck Institute for Plasmaphysics in Munich-Garching, a highly competent scientific institution. The fact that they were authorized to participate in the investigation and make an official report on it (which is in my possession) is proof of a broad-mindedness that is extremely rare among "established" scientists.

Furthermore, established science, the police, the electric supply company, and German television showed absolutely remarkable understanding and breadth of vision in this matter. The police even accepted a complaint against "X," but to date have not arrested any "spirit."

It is true that the phenomenon occurred not in a castle of dubious and accursed repute, but in the office of a German attorney, the least frivolous of all possible places. Nevertheless, it is very difficult to draw any conclusions.

Minor psychokinetic effects in which the human will seems to act on matter appear to have been noted by some investigators (other investigators deny it). But such an effect involving a one-foot shift of an object weighing 385 pounds has never been observed in a laboratory or elsewhere.

If there does exist an unknown force emanating from the human mind and acting on matter, it can also act on electrons, which are materials, and thus produce an electric current. Or it can act on the springs of an automatic telephone dial, or on the needle of a measuring instrument.

The Rosenheim force produced phenomena which, according to Professor Bender, "had to be directed by intelligence with precise technical knowledge, capable of estimating intervals with a duration of milliseconds."

This is what is new and terrifying about the Rosenheim phenomenon—it represents a *step forward* over similar phenomena.

Is another life, electrical in nature, being born and developing alongside of our life? Will it one day take over our machines, as in Theodore Sturgeon's terrifying novel, *Killdozer*?

# THE BURNING PEOPLE
## Ronald J. Willis

*The spontaneous combustion, for no apparent reason, of human beings or objects involves the problem of the "secret fire." According to the alchemists, there may exist a type of fire different from the one we know, and which may be extremely dangerous. In terms of modern physics, this phenomenon could be interpreted as being halfway between chemical energy and nuclear energy. This article by Ronald J. Willis is an excellent contribution to studies of this type.*

The landlady carried a telegram to the door of Mrs. Reeser's apartment in St. Petersburg, Florida. She knocked three times and waited. There was no answer, so she knocked again. Still no answer. She tried the door. The doorknob was hot, which reminded her of the slight smell of smoke she had noticed earlier. But the smell had disappeared and she hadn't called the fire department. After knocking again several times, she called the police who came and knocked down the door. A strange sight met them.

In the middle of the apartment, an overstuffed chair had been burned down to its metal springs. There was seen soot on the ceiling and a charred spot in the carpet around the chair, but otherwise it had been only a small fire. But where was Mrs. Reeser? On advancing to the chair, the police found what was left of her. Her head was there—charred black and shriveled to the size of a baseball. They found also a bit of her spine and a small part of one foot. That was all, save a few gray ashes on and around the chair.

The coroner was astounded. How could a fire so small that it had merely burnt up the stuffings of one chair, and hardly been noticed elsewhere in the house, so thoroughly consume a human body? Dr. Wilton Krogman, international expert in death by fire at Pennsylvania's School of Medicine, was vacationing nearby and was called in. "It's the most anazing thing I've ever seen," said Dr. Krogman. "I cannot conceive of such complete cremation without more burning of the apartment itself. In fact, the apartment and everything in it should have been consumed. Never have I seen a human skull shrunk by intense heat. The opposite has always been true, the skulls either have been abnormally swollen or have virtually exploded into hundreds of pieces."

The police considered suicide, accident, and murder, but there was no motive found for her death. Above all there was no known means by which Mrs. Reeser could have been killed the way she was. It takes a heat of 2,500 degrees Fahrenheit about three hours to consume a body to this extent—ask anyone at a crematorium.

A single weird, unexplained death of an old woman? No, just another in a long series of deaths often called by the old-fashioned name "spontaneous combustion." For hundreds of years, medical men have reported cases of the human body bursting into flames or being found fantastically charred with no indication of how this could have happened. Often the surrounding area is totally unharmed, showing that the tremendous heat was somehow limited mostly to the body itself. This limitation of the heat to the immediate surroundings is one of the most mysterious aspects of the phenomenon.

Take the case of the Rooneys. They lived in a farmhouse near

Seneca, Illinois. On Christmas Eve, 1885, Patrick Rooney, his wife, and their hired man John Larson were drinking whiskey in the kitchen. Larson went to bed and woke up Christmas morning sick. Downstairs in the kitchen he found everything covered with an oily film, and on the floor—Patrick Rooney, dead. Larson rodé to get help from Rooney's son John, who lived nearby. Back at the farm, the two men noticed that there was a charred hole next to the kitchen table. Looking into the hole, they found lying on the earth under the kitchen floor, a calcined skull, a few charred bones, and a pile of ashes. The coroner found that Patrick had been suffocated by the smoke of the burning body of his wife. The coroner's jury came up with no verdict. Mrs. Rooney had been obliterated by a fantastically hot fire that had not spread beyond her immediate area. It was beyond the understanding of this jury of midwestern farmers in the nineteenth century.

Dr. Dixon Mann, in a book on forensic medicine, lists some combustion cases. One involved a woman who was found on the floor of her room a pile of charred bones, but with a tablecloth only three feet away undamaged. Mann, like many earlier writers on spontaneous combustion, thought that all the victims drank very heavily, and that somehow, dowsing one's insides with alcohol could lead it to burst into flame. Some of the victims were heavy drinkers, but some of them were teetotalers, and the alcohol theory is obviously not adequate.

Eric Frank Russell, the English writer and investigator of strange events, found nineteen cases of spontaneous combustion in humans in the papers just in the year 1938, and this was no doubt only a small part of the cases actually occurring. The most spectacular case was from Chelmsford, England, in which a woman in the middle of a dance floor suddenly burst into bright blue flames and in only minutes was a pile of charred ashes. The coroner said, "In all my experience I have never come across a case as mysterious as this."

Curiously enough Russell found a sinister "rule of three" in some of these events. On December 27, 1938, a woman was consumed at Downham, Kentucky, and another at Brixton, then a man in Balina, Ireland. None of these people were near any fire, or smoked.

Even more sinister were the three deaths of April 7, 1938. Aboard the freighter S.S. *Ulrich* off the coast of Ireland, the mate noticed the vessel was yawing, and found the helmsman, John Greeley, gone. Only a pile of ashes lay in front of the wheel. There were no signs of fire—the wheel, the compass, the floor, even the shoes of the dead man were unharmed. Other seamen had been working on the deck nearby but no one had heard any cry or noise of any kind. A lightning bolt was suggested, but the sky had been clear and no one else had heard any noise at all.

Again on April 7, near Upton-by-Chester, England, a truck rolled to a stop in a ditch. Police investigating found the driver, George Turner, had been incinerated. Yet even the cushions of the cab were unharmed! The gas tank was intact, there had been no fire in the cab save in the body of the driver himself.

And third, on April 7, near Nijmegen, Holland, William ten Bruik was found dead, "burned beyond recognition" in his Volkswagen. Yet damage to the car was slight, and the gas tank had not ignited. Again there was no explanation for the incineration of ten Bruik.

Why were these three deaths of Greeley, Turner, and ten Bruik so sinister? They had occurred over an area hundreds of miles apart, but—they had occurred at the exact same time! This suggests some connection between these three bizarre deaths, even though separated by such distances.

Why are scientists wary of getting involved with cases of spontaneous combustion? Partly because their extent is not fully realized, since many cases may not be reported to the newspapers, and scientific journals rarely report such cases. To the scientist and medical researcher, these cases must smack of some sort of medieval superstition—so they refuse to investigate.

Some possible connection with the bizarre and occult is supported by the case of Peter Vesey. Vesey had long written "astrological fiction" and dabbled with the occult. He worked alone in his study on an isolated farm in the west. Because he was working on some special project at the time, he asked his wife and son to take a walk for an hour or so so he could be completely alone with his work. Upon returning, they found on the floor of the living room the crisp and charred remains of Peter Vesey. Nothing else was burned at all. A small fire was burning in the fireplace at the far end of the room, but there could have been no connection between it and Vesey's death.

But on and on the tally of cases can be made. A couple of recent ones: In 1960 near Pikeville, Kentucky, five men were found in a burnt car on a lonely road. The coroner said the charred bodies were "sitting there as though they'd just gotten into the car. With all that heat, it seems there'd been some sort of struggle to try to escape. But there hadn't been." No indications were found of any foul play. In April 1970, Grace Walker of Long Beach, California, was found terribly burned in her house—her clothes in ashes around her. She was dead on arrival at the hospital.

There is another case in INFO's files involving a car, which unfortunately is not dated but is from the past ten years. Jacques Bergier contributed this clipping which states that Leon Eveille, forty years old, was found burnt to a crisp in his Simca auto in a pine woods near d'Arcis-sur-Aube, France. The strange thing about the case is that the windows of the car were totally *melted*. Now a burning car rarely generates a heat above 700 degrees centigrade. But glass only melts at about 1000 degrees centigrade. No one had any explanation for the intense flames that liquified the glass. Curiously perhaps, a Mr. Reveille in 1954 saw, about twenty kilometers from where this case took place, a luminous object giving off an intense heat. Even though it was raining heavily, the place where the object had been sitting before taking off was dry for a half-hour thereafter because of the heat of the ground.

Does anyone escape this strange phenomena that burns people to death in a short time? Perhaps. Paul V. Weekley of Sioux City, Iowa, awoke early one morning to find his bed aflame. He put it out, went to sleep, and an hour later his bed flamed again. No possible explanation could be found for this fire, the sheet, quilt, and bedspread being brand new. Did Weekley narrowly miss a terrible end?

Then there is the strange case of an unnamed professor from

the University of Nashville. Sometime before 1835, the professor one day took a walk and returned to his room. While he was noting down the reading of his meteorological instruments, he felt a stinging on his left leg. He slapped and rubbed it to make it stop, but the pain increased. Looking at his trouser leg, he found a flame burning there about the size of a dime. He cupped his hands over it to keep out the oxygen and it soon went out. He took off his pants and found a spot three inches long, from which the skin had peeled. The underwear had been burnt through at this spot, but the pants were hardly touched. The burn on the leg healed very slowly. It was called at the time "partial spontaneous combustion."

Sometimes the burn victims live awhile before dying. In 1943, Madge Knight of Sussex, England, awakened the household with her screams. She was lying in bed, covered by bedclothes, but with her back terribly burned. There was no trace of fire on the sheets. Doctors treated her, but she died some time later. Though repeatedly asked what had happened, the poor woman could only say that she didn't know.

In nineteenth-century London, the mother of John Wright was burnt as she sat with a servant girl before a small fire in the hearth. The fire in her clothes was extinguished but later the same thing happened. Again the clothes were extinguished, but the next day she was found in the kitchen a living torch. Put to bed, she was again surrounded by flames. Wright blamed the girl for the happenings, but his mother denied it. She said that "something supernatural" was attacking her.

The *Shreveport Times*, of November 18, 1880, carried an amazing story under the heading "Attacked by an Electric Flame." We quote:

A San Antonio special of the 12th to the Galveston News says: Yesterday evening Fred Bader, 11 years old, son of Constable Bader, went home from school and found his parents gone. He went to the cupboard to slice off a piece of bread, buttered it, then went to the front of the house, sat down on a gate post and began eating. In a few seconds he was enveloped in a flame which passed around the house to an irrigation ditch and was lost. Freddie's sister, nearby, saw the flame and described it as a ball of fire. Freddie's hat was burned, also his shirt, bosom, and his eyebrows singed off, and the hair, where not protected by the hat.

Today he is unable to see and can scarcely hear. His face is swollen and ridged as if by a sharp instrument. The boy is in great pain and may lose both sight and hearing. There was no one near him except his little nine-year-old sister at the time. The burning is said by physicians to have been produced by electric fire.

The number of spontaneous combustion cases, even though not well publicized, are many. See Charles Fort's *Wild Talents* (New York: Holt, 1941). Vincent Gaddis's *Mysterious Fires and Lights* (New York: McKay, 1967), and Eric Frank Russell's *Great World Mysteries* (New York: Mayflower-Dell, 1967) for more cases. But many cases are not included in these works. Allen M. Small, aged 82, was found dead in his home in Deer Isle, Maine, January 13, 1943. Fire had burned off the clothing from the upper part of the body, the carpet under the body was charred, and the room was "in confusion," but nothing else was burned. His pipe was on the shelf, and the stove was in order. What had killed him and why hadn't the fire spread?

February 1, 1943, Arthur Baugard, aged 39, an invalid, was found burned beyond recognition in Lancaster, New York. Investigators could not understand why the fire hadn't spread, but had only consumed the body.

From the *New York Times*, July 5, 1959, comes the story of Mrs. Edward Mottern who was found dead of burns in her penthouse on East 57th Street. Mr. Mottern had smelled smoke as he slept in the bedroom and came out to find his wife burnt to death, the chair "smouldering," but apparently no other damage to the apartment nor any indication of what had happened.

On June 1, 1966, the *St. Louis Post-Dispatch* reported that Mrs. Ethel Woodward, aged 68, was found dead in her burning bed in St. Louis. The lady did not smoke and no cause for the fire was found. Firemen were clearly mystified as to why the damage was so slight.

The *Palo Alto Times* of November 16, 1966, has an interesting case. Marlin Stevens Smith, aged 54, was found near his bed, which had been destroyed by fire. It is not clear that Smith died of severe burns since an autopsy was being conducted to determine the cause of death. Authorities could not understand why the fire in the bed had gone out apparently after Smith left it.

The listing of these cases can be continued indefinitely, but in the end what can be the explanation of these terrible and deadly attacks? Often the authorities try to blame it on an open fire or smoking igniting clothing or bedding. But in almost all these cases, this is clearly an "explanation" advanced to get the authorities off the hook, since they really have no idea of what causes the phenomenon. The victims are often nonsmokers, the fire is often far from the body, and in modern days, there is rarely an open fire around. Nineteenth-century writers claimed many of the victims were drunkards, assuming that a human impregnated with alcohol would more earily burn up. Yet attempts to impregnate animal tissue with large amounts of alcohol showed that it was virtually impossible to get it to burn at all, much less burn at the fantastic heat of 2,500 degrees Fahrenheit necessary to incinerate flesh and bone. But there may be some strange biochemical situation that can arise in the human body that can lead to such burning. The case of the Nashville professor indicates that this is a possibility, but we have absolutely no idea what the conditions would be.

Is there any possibility that some of these cases are suicides—psychic suicides? Many of the cases involved older people, especially women, who may have felt alone and bypassed in life. Is it possible that similarly to the Lung-Gompa, the Buddhist ascetics alleged to be able to sit in the snow and melt it for eight feet around them, these people can subconsciously energize in their body the ability to annihilate themselves?

Cade and Davis's *Taming of the Thunderbolts* lists many cases of "ball lightning," which sometimes injures and kills humans. The conventional scientific explanation for this, which is now accepted, is that it is some sort of plasma phenomenon. Yet many of the cases of ball lightning themselves display very puzzling behavior. It would appear that spontaneous combustion cases are not in general related to ball lightning since the "thunderbolts" usually coincide with thunderstorms, and if it were possible to use this explanation for the burning people, it would surely have been done so by the authorities who dislike mysteries on their books. Only the case of Fred Bader above sounds as though it might have been caused by ball lightning.

There is apparently no actual case recorded in which UFOs of any type were related to the burnings by any investigator. In *Wild Talents*, Fort lists cases that were related to poltergeist phenomena. The cases in which the body is burned but not the clothes are particularly difficult to explain.

Few of the cases in our collection, or from any of the authors cited, seem particularly concerned with the meteorological conditions at the time of these burnings. Only the Greeley case noted weather conditions at the time. If there were a thunderstorm, it could have been dragged in to supply lightning for an explanation. There may be no connection with any meteorological condition at any rate, but only broader data would indicate this.

Yet perhaps the explanation of these cases is as weird as one can imagine. In describing Russell's cases, Michael MacDougall says of the three victims incinerated on April 7, 1938, "It was as if a galactic being of unimaginable size had probed Earth with a three-tined fork, three fingers of fire which burned only flesh."

Is it possible that there are strange sentient fire beings that swoop down on certain individuals and incinerate them mysteriously? Remember Mrs. Wright who said something "supernatural" was attacking her. What possible motivation these creatures could have is beyond our imagination, but then much of the universe is still beyond our ken. It's not a pleasant thing to think about when going to bed late tonight!

# THE HAUNTED RECTORY
# OF BORLEY

## Jacques Bergier

*Of all the cases discussed in the present book, that of the haunted rectory of Borley is the only one with a logical explanation. There is a good reason for this, but it is so unexpected, and the ending has such a strong resemblance to endings of the best detective stories, that the story of the haunted rectory of Borley could have been written by Agatha Christie.*

*All of the facts discussed below, including the incredible final ending, are completely authentic.*

Let us begin with the legend.

In the thirteenth century, in the English countryside, there stood a monastery and convent. A monk ran away with a nun, was caught, and was killed. The nun, the carriage in which she and the monk were captured, and a headless coachman appeared in the form of ghosts for centuries thereafter.

In the nineteenth century, this spot in Essex County became the

159

site of a rectory built in 1863 by the Reverend Henry D. E. Bull. This pious man lived peaceably there with his wife and fourteen children, without experiencing any particular problems. His son succeeded him as vicar. On July 28, 1900, the nun's ghost was seen, but aside from this, all was calm—the calm before the storm.

On October 2, 1928, the Reverend Eric Smith was appointed to the Borley rectory. In 1929, feeling that the place was haunted, he wrote to his newspaper, the *Daily Mirror*. On June 10, 1929, the *Daily Mirror* sent Harry Price, the famous ghost hunter, to investigate. On June 12, 1929, the trouble began. Stones and other objects were thrown. The maid saw apparitions. The terrified Reverend Smith left Borley. On October 16, 1930, after the rectory had been without an occupant for six months, the church authorities appointed another minister, the Reverend Lionel A. Foyster.

Then the terror began. For two years, phenomena proliferated in every form. In January, 1932, exorcism was tried—a rather bizarre type of exorcism, however, since it was performed by a spiritualist group. This calmed the "spirits" slightly, but they soon began acting up again. In May, 1937, Harry Price announced his intention of getting to the bottom of the matter, and moved into the rectory, bringing with him several spiritualists who made contact with the murdered nun, a Frenchwoman named Marie Lairre. The phenomena resumed, more actively than before.

The apotheosis occurred at midnight on February 27, 1939, when the haunted rectory caught fire and burned to the ground. Witnesses of the fire saw strange, nonhuman beings walking in the flames. After this splendid finale, a few small phenomena occurred.

In 1943, Price found buried human bones, which were presumed to be those of the nun.

In 1944, a brick rose from the ruins and hurled itself at Price, just missing him.

Groups consisting of dozens of ghost and spirit hunters wandered about in the accursed ruins.

In 1948, Harry Price died. In the same year the extraordinary truth came out: *It was Harry Price himself, the great ghost hunter, who had created all the phenomena.* In a twist reminiscent of those detective stories in which the detective is the criminal, it was Harry Price who had thrown bricks, made noises, struck blows, and then very probably started the fire.

Harry Price knew by 1938 that the legend of the nun was a pure fiction invented in the sixteenth century. He had been supplied with categorical proofs but had refrained from making them public. Witnesses were found who had seen him rapping and throwing bricks. Nothing was left of the legend.

This hurt many people. Doctor Paul Vasse wrote, "It seems clear . . . that Harry Price exaggerated, cheated, and mutilated evidence, seeking sensationalism at any price. But perhaps, as is suggested at the end of this book with undue timidity, he wanted to supply the finishing touch, the finishing touch of sufficient power to force the phenomenon."

Plainly put, this kind of finishing touch is called trickery. What is extraordinary is the manner in which the legend grew. Obviously Price is responsible for this, but peoples' desire to believe at any price also bears a major share of the responsibility.

For years, impartial witnesses had been calling attention to the presence of numerous rats in the Borley rectory, but no attention was paid to them. One of these skeptical witnesses, the driver of a bus transporting a group of spiritualists, did something brilliant when the Reverend Bull was invoked. Concealing himself in the shadows, he cried out in a guttural voice, "Reverend Bull is dead, and you're all crazy." This incident was revealed only much later, after the legend had been demolished. But not until the appearance of the definitive book on the rectory of Borley by Eric J. Dingwall, Kathleen M. Goldney, and Trevor H. Hall was the truth finally established.

As early as 1949, however, numerous witnesses had declared that Price was the perpetrator of the hoax. Yet even today books are still being written in which the Borley rectory is referred to as "the most haunted house in England."

The lesson to be learned from this story is that when dealing with parapsychology we must be wary of everything and everybody. We of the twentieth century are not the only people who invent stories; a great number of legends are pure inventions. This does not mean that all phenomena are false. Two other articles in this book, concerning the accursed hospital of Arcachon and the electric ghost of Rosenheim, involve phenomena whose existence has been fully established.

In the case of Borley, we are dealing with both a legend on which everyone embroidered and an unscrupulous individual who developed it into numerous books, documentaries, and television and radio broadcasts. It is possible that a certain number of practical jokers had already been active at Borley before Price. A careful study has been made of the adventures of small groups of spiritualists and ghost hunters, varying in number from four to twelve, who had wandered around Borley. In numerous cases, it is very evident how the suggestion was born and spread, and from the psychological point of view these various documents are of tremendous interest.

Another very interesting aspect of the Borley affair is the fact that some people were ready to believe absolutely anything. Thus, a jacket left there by a workman who had come to clean the house, and which was later identified, was deemed to have been brought there paranormally. Four witnesses had seen it materialize! After that, it is not astonishing that creatures had been seen walking in the flames during the fire.

What is quite surprising is the fact that no flying saucer ever landed at Borley. This is probably because the flying saucers began to appear in force in 1949, while Price died in 1948. But for this, he could have created a landing strip for flying saucers in Borley. But strange lights were seen in Borley that were perhaps position lights of flying saucers. It was also said that the well of the rectory contained the Holy Grail. Why not? It should also be noted that events were organized at Borley that today would be called "happenings," but at that time were called "psychic festivals."

The *Suffolk Free Press*, to which I leave the responsibility for the statement, says that in 1942, during one of these festivals, the legendary ghostly carriage had been seen at Borley in broad daylight, complete with its occupants in the costumes of the period, going to the rectory. It then rose into the air and disintegrated, with limbs, wheels, and other parts falling in every direction!

There was also a story about a woman who visited Borley, and whose wedding ring was torn off her finger. A ghostly stagecoach had been heard traveling along the lane.

More than thirty people heard invisible bells ringing in a corridor that does not appear on the plan of Borley.

On April 27, 1941, a spiritualist investigator, Mr. S. L. Croft, lost a pencil at Borley. According to him this pencil was taken away to the other world, and he supplied a description of it, just in case it should be involved in any phenomena.

In 1947, another investigator left his raincoat near the cemetery wall. In his absence, someone sat on it.

In the cases of a number of witnesses, we do not know what they saw because they would only reveal it for a modest sum of money. Some of them would have been satisfied with a guinea, which is very little when you think of the couple in the United States who were abducted by flying saucers, and collected $50,000 from a weekly newspaper.

Then there is the case of a group of students who organized an apparition on the lawn. It was described in detail in spiritualist reports.

There was also a ghostly dog, but it was shot to death by the inhabitants in 1952.

A systematic search was made of the cellars, where batteries, wiring, electric bulbs, and all the equipment needed to provide for ghostly lights were found. (Unless, of course, these batteries themselves came from the other world.)

In conclusion, here are a few details supplied by a witness concerning the bricks that flew through the ruins.

"As I told you at our first meeting one year ago, I myself had occasion to observe the most shameless trickery on the part of the late Harry Price. In April, 1944, he took Mr. David Scherman and me to Borley. Mr. Price's version of what happened can be found in *E.B.R.*, page 284. He speaks of a mysterious *flying brick* photographed by Mr. Scherman. As he says, there was no string or wire attached to it. What he doesn't say is that a strong workman was still working behind the wall—all three of us saw him when we passed near the house to take the photograph. There is absolutely no doubt that the flying bricks, several of which appeared at regular intervals, were thrown by this workman during his demolition work."

To conclude: Absolute distrust is absolutely necessary when dealing with the paranormal. Because this rule has not been observed in most cases, the existence of the paranormal is rejected by many serious thinkers who have been discouraged by affairs of the Borley type.

The story of Borley rectory has a moral, and it is this: While systematic denial is as harmful for research as the most naive credulity, doubt and distrust are absolutely necessary. We must always be wary, we must always check. Ninety-nine out of one hundred cases will break down, but the one hundredth case should be retained and can be utilized.

This is what Charles Fort himself sought, and this is what we have all tried to do in this book.